Kasi Lemmons: Interviews

Conversations with Filmmakers Series
Gerald Perry, General Editor

KASI
LEMMONS

INTERVIEWS

Edited by Christina N. Baker

University Press of Mississippi / Jackson

The University Press of Mississippi is the scholarly publishing agency of
the Mississippi Institutions of Higher Learning: Alcorn State University,
Delta State University, Jackson State University, Mississippi State University,
Mississippi University for Women, Mississippi Valley State University,
University of Mississippi, and University of Southern Mississippi.

www.upress.state.ms.us

The University Press of Mississippi is a member
of the Association of University Presses.

First printing 2021
∞

Library of Congress Cataloging-in-Publication Data

Names: Lemmons, Kasi, interviewee. | Baker, Christina N., editor.
Title: Kasi Lemmons: Interviews / edited by Christina N. Baker.
Other titles: Conversations with Filmmakers series.
Description: Jackson: University Press of Mississippi, 2021. | Series:
  Conversations with Filmmakers series | Includes bibliographical
  references and index.
Identifiers: LCCN 2020032148 (print) | LCCN 2020032149 (ebook) | ISBN
  978-1-4968-3168-2 (hardback) | ISBN 978-1-4968-3169-9 (trade paperback) | ISBN
  978-1-4968-3170-5 (epub) | ISBN 978-1-4968-3167-5 (epub) | ISBN 978-1-4968-3171-2
  (pdf) | ISBN 978-1-4968-3172-9 (pdf)
Subjects: LCSH: Lemmons, Kasi—Interviews. | Motion picture producers and
  directors—United States—Interviews. | African American motion picture
  producers and directors—Interviews. | African American women motion
  picture producers and directors—Interviews.
Classification: LCC PN1998.3.L4574 A5 2021 (print) | LCC PN1998.3.L4574
  (ebook) | DDC 791.4302/33092 [B—dc23
LC record available at https://lccn.loc.gov/2020032148
LC ebook record available at https://lccn.loc.gov/2020032149

British Library Cataloging-in-Publication Data available

Contents

Introduction

Artist. Activist. Black Feminist. For filmmaker Kasi Lemmons, the significance of these identities is unmistakable in the enduring body of work that she has created. The collection of interviews in this book illuminates Kasi Lemmons's distinctive ability through film, her chosen medium of artistic expression, to actualize stories that broaden social expectations of cinematic Black femaleness and maleness. As Lemmons explains in an interview, "At a certain point I realized—and it became my mission, because it was also just inherently true—that all of my art is protest art. It was protesting against something and it didn't matter if the reader or the audience knew exactly what I was protesting against, but there was always a form of protest art. I felt that me, myself as an artist, this Black woman artist, was already a statement."[1]

I had the privilege and pleasure of interviewing Kasi Lemmons about her transformative work as well as the personal connection that she has to the art she creates. Our conversation is included in this collection of interviews. This book also includes Lemmons's interviews with scholars, writers, journalists, and filmmakers Susan Bullington Katz, Erika Muhammad, Annie Nocenti, Cynthia Fuchs, Wheeler Winston Dixon, Sarah Kuhn, Melissa Silverstein, Melinda Loewenstein, Rachel Martin, Natalie Chang, Janell Hobson, Joi-Marie McKenzie, Daniel Joyaux, and Peppur Chambers. What is apparent in these conversations is that Lemmons's passion for creating art through film is intimately linked to her mission to protest culturally and structurally-imposed limitations and push the boundaries of the film industry, from her critically acclaimed independent film debut *Eve's Bayou* (1997) to her blockbuster film *Harriet* (2019).

From Actor to Artist

"I'm an artist. I know my history, I know my roots, I know I can be an artist. Of course I'm a minority, but that makes it interesting."[2] As a filmmaker, Lemmons has stayed true to her artistic vision, and problematized what film scholar Ed Guerrero describes as "Hollywood's unceasing efforts to frame blackness."[3] As a writer-director, Kasi Lemmons has experienced the triumphs and challenges of being a Black woman in Hollywood whose artistry is behind the camera. However, her experiences in front of the camera inspired her to become a filmmaker.

Lemmons brings an exceptional perspective to directing, that of an experienced screen actor, with roles in numerous television series and feature films, including Spike Lee's socially significant *School Daze* (1988) and Jonathan Demme's Academy Award winner, *The Silence of the Lambs* (1991). Although acting was her first love, she was unfulfilled, recognizing that she didn't have creative control. In her interview with Erika Muhammad, Lemmons says, "As an actress I couldn't empty my soul because the parts I was playing would not allow that sort of artistic relief: Black Girl Best Friend, Black Girl Next Door, Black Girl Cop. I was frustrated and I had this story inside me."

Taking film courses at The New School in Manhattan resulted from her frustration with the marginalization and limitations experienced by African American actresses in Hollywood. "I wanted to do something more meaningful than going to auditions, waiting for auditions or waiting for the phone to ring. I thought that I should really learn to make films."[4] At the New School, she developed her talent to create films from *her point of view*, to insert her voice and vision.

Eve's Bayou as Artistic Expression and Activism

"If it is not nominated for Academy Awards, then the Academy is not paying attention,"[5] said film critic Roger Ebert of *Eve's Bayou* (1997), Lemmons's first feature film, which she wrote and directed. Not only was this debut film critically successful, but *Eve's Bayou* was among the highest grossing independent films of the year. Moreover, the enduring cultural impact of *Eve's Bayou* is evidenced by the fact that, in 2018, the film was added to the Library of Congress's National Film Registry as a culturally, historically, or aesthetically significant film.

However, Lemmons did not write *Eve's Bayou* for the Academy, nor for audiences or critics. She wrote *Eve's Bayou* for herself—for the personal liberation and sense of fulfilment that came from the process of expressing part of herself through writing the story. As Lemmons explains in her interview with Susan Bullington Katz, "I felt definitely liberated by the fact that I wasn't planning on showing it to anybody. I didn't care if anybody liked it. It made me laugh and cry. And I would sit there and cry and laugh, and that was really what I needed to get out of it, and I didn't really need anything else. All the rest has been icing." She echoes this sentiment in her interview with Annie Nocenti, in advice to other writers: "Write from your heart, completely for yourself, as if nobody else is ever going to see it." Despite the personal nature of *Eve's Bayou* for Lemmons, or perhaps *because* of it, her artistic vision resonated with the movie-going audience when it was released. "It was just really beautiful that the story found its way into other people's hearts," she expresses in her interview with Wheeler Winston Dixon.

Eve's Bayou's focus on an affluent, predominantly female Creole family living in rural Louisiana was so successfully accomplished that it threatened "essentialist notions of black experience as definitely urban, ghetto-centered, and youth-culture dominated," asserts film scholar Mia Mask. [6] Lemmons created a seemingly autonomous world of complex African American female characters, where being Black was an unquestioned and unproblematic part of one's existence. It was a form of protest for Lemmons to make a film that reflected her vision as a Black woman in Hollywood, and that was wedded to her own experiences.[7] Lemmons's vision and experience meant that *Eve's Bayou* would have an entirely African American cast. She discusses this subtle but powerful form of activism in an interview with Cynthia Fuchs: "It was very important that it was one hundred percent African American, because these are the people of Eve's life. People asked me to put in white characters, and I would say, 'Well, there aren't any. It's my bayou.' To me that had its own power and stirred things up."

Persistence in the Face of Resistance

"It's still very, very difficult to get an African American film made," Lemmons told Wheeler Winston Dixon in her 2006 interview. "At the studio level, we don't quite have the executives we need. And then, when they are in there, they have to do what they think is going to help them keep their job and what makes sense for their company. Studios feel that African American movies don't sell overseas, for whatever reason, and they feel that the black films will sell only to a certain segment of the population, and that's it."

Lemmons broke the mold of what is expected of a filmmaker. She described to an interviewer, Sarah Kuhn, the prototypical film director as "25 to 45 and has that kind of scruffy, slightly rumpled look . . . And he's a white man . . . I do not fit that aesthetic." But Lemmons remained intensely true to her artistic vision. "I had a big dream that I was very intent on vigorously fulfilling . . . That's the way I lived it," she told interviewer, Natalie Chang. Lemmons pledged "to keep doing movies that are challenging stories and have a certain degree of not-your-average-movieness."[8]

After *Eve's Bayou*, Lemmons directed the films *The Caveman's Valentine* (2001) and *Talk to Me* (2007), and each challenged cultural ideology related to cinematic Blackness. *The Caveman's Valentine* is based on a novel about an African American, Julliard-trained pianist who has schizophrenia and is homeless. *The Caveman's Valentine* is referred to by its director as "a bigger film than *Eve's Bayou*"[9] and, as it deals with a population that is disenfranchised and often dismissed, "much, much riskier."[10] Lemmons reiterated this point with Cynthia Fuchs during their interview: "I knew I was pushing a lot of buttons."

Talk to Me (2007) is a fictionalized account of Ralph Waldo "Petey" Greene, a well-known Black radio talk show host and community activist during the 1960s, and his friendship with his manager, Dewey Hughes. In an interview about the film, Lemmons explains her intention was to break down myths about Black maleness: "I wanted to get inside a relationship between two men where they could be vulnerable and need each other. I feel that it's real, and yet men are very afraid of showing emotion and being demonstrative. It helps us to understand men more when we realize they are capable of these friendships."[11] Like her previous films, the multidimensional Black characters in *Talk to Me* call into question dominant cultural views of racial and gender identity.

After *The Caveman's Valentine* and *Talk to Me*, Lemmons returned to her role as writer-director for *Black Nativity* (2013). *Black Nativity* is a holiday musical film with an African American cast based on a Langston Hughes play of the same name. As this film celebrates the work of Hughes, one of the most significant African American literary and cultural figures in history, it also continues Lemmons's goal of creating films that "have a certain degree of not-your-average-movieness." *Black Nativity* was described by one film critic as successfully "dispelling the idea that Christmas musicals need Bing Crosby in a Santa hat."[12] To further emphasize her approach of telling a Christmas story that is not limited by antiquated cultural expectations, as she says to interviewer Melinda Loewenstein, "I wanted to make a contemporary story that would feel very relevant and very real about the problems facing families and especially in the African American community."

Black Feminism and the Future of Filmmaking

Lemmons directed and co-wrote the high-profile *Harriet* (2019), the first theatrical feature film about iconic abolitionist and activist Harriet Tubman. It was a resounding hit, earning over $40 million at the box office (as of January 2020). *New York Times* film critic A.O. Scott praised *Harriet* as "a rousing and powerful drama, respectful of both the historical record and the cravings of modern audiences. The story of Tubman's escape from enslavement on a Maryland farm and her subsequent leadership in the underground railroad is conveyed in bold, emphatic strokes."

Interviewer Janell Hobson asked Lemmons if she'd made a Black feminist film: "Absolutely. It has to be. I don't understand how you could really be living in these times and be a black woman and not be a black feminist," said the filmmaker. Lemmons's Black feminist perspective is further emphasized during her interview with Peppur Chambers, when she describes her artistic choice to add the friendship between Harriet and another Black woman, Marie, to the film: "One moment that I love is this wonderful friendship between Harriet and Marie . . . it became very important to me."

In an interview with Natalie Chang, Lemmons brings feminism home, discussing her own strategy to address the status and underrepresentation of women in filmmaking. "What are we going to do about women working in the industry? My way of dealing with it is to teach,"[13] explains Lemmons. Presently, she is an Associate Arts Professor at New York University's Tisch School of the Arts, where she continues to challenge racial and gender ideology through mentoring and teaching others. "It's gratifying because you feel like you're changing the world, you're changing the landscape," she states.[14] She is inspiring young artists, many of them women and people of color, to make their mark and disrupt cinematic and cultural expectations in their own way.

Lemmons's own career as an artist-activist is encapsulated by an insight that she shares in an interview with Melissa Silverstein: "Find a way of telling a story that represents an aspect of you, so you can use it as a calling card to help shape your identity so someone else doesn't put you in a box. Create something or find a piece of material that is a love letter to yourself." From *Eve's Bayou* to *Harriet*, Lemmons's films represent an activist's love letter to herself, to aspiring artists, and to Black women.

Notes

1. Joi-Marie McKenzie, "Eve's Bayou Screenwriter Kasi Lemmons Says Black Women Writers Have a Responsibility," *Essence Magazine*, February 5, 2019. https://www.essence.com/entertainment/the-writers -room/eves-bayou-screenwriter-kasi-lemmons-says-black-woman-writers-have-a-responsibility/.

2. Natalie Chang, "Third Act: The Journey of a Hollywood Director," *The Atlantic Magazine*, 2016, https://www.theatlantic.com/sponsored/forevermark-2016/third-act-the-journey-of-a-hollywood-dire ctor/816/. Accessed July 10, 2019.

3. Ed Guerrero, *Framing Blackness: The African American Image in Film* (Philadelphia: Temple University Press, 1993).

4. George Alexander, *Why We Make Movies: Black Filmmakers Talk about the Magic of Cinema* (Harlem Moon, 2003).

5. Roger Ebert, "Eve's Bayou Movie Review & Film Summary (1997)," *Rogerebert.com*, November 7, 1997, http://www.rogerebert.com/reviews/eves-bayou-1997.

6. Mia Mask, "Eve's Bayou: Too Good to Be a 'Black' Film?," *Cineaste* 23, no. 4 (December 1998): 26.

7. Though some of the setting and characters in *Eve's Bayou* were inspired by Lemmons's experiences, the film is not autobiographical.

8. Cynthia Fuchs, "Caveman's Valentine: I Just Like to Stir It Up a Little—Interview with Kasi Lemmons," *NitrateOnline.com*, March 9, 2001, http://www.nitrateonline.com/2001/fcaveman.html.

9. Fuchs.

10. Wheeler Winston Dixon, *Film Talk: Directors at Work* (New Brunswick, NJ: Rutgers University Press, 2007).

11. Melissa Silverstein, *In Her Voice: Women Directors Talk Directing* (Open Road Distribution, 2015).

12. Patrick Fahy, "Black Nativity," *Sight & Sound* 24, no. 2 (February 2014): 76–77.

13. Natalie Chang, "Third Act: The Journey of a Hollywood Director," *The Atlantic Magazine*, 2016, https://www.theatlantic.com/sponsored/forevermark-2016/third-act-the-journey-of-a-hollywood-director/816/. Accessed July 10, 2019.

14. Christina N. Baker, *Contemporary Black Women Filmmakers and the Art of Resistance* (Columbus: The Ohio State University Press, 2018).

Chronology

1961	Born February 24 in St. Louis, Missouri, as Karen Lemmons.
1970–78	Parents divorce. Moves to Massachusetts with mother and two sisters. Begins drama class at Boston Children's Theatre, through which she acquired her first professional television acting role on a local show called *You Got a Right*. Attends Commonwealth High School in Massachusetts and Circle in the Square Theatre School during the summer in New York City.
1979–84	Attends college at New York University's Tisch School of the Arts. Transfers to University of California, Los Angeles. Works as an actor in several commercials. First film acting job is in the 1979 television movie *11th Victim*.
1984–89	Moves back to New York. Attends film school at The New School in Manhattan. Works with the Steppenwolf Theatre Company at the Minetta Lane Theatre in New York with John Malkovich as director. Appears in an Off-Broadway production of *Balm in Gilead* in 1984. Acting roles in multiple television series: *Spencer: For Hire*, *As the World Turns*, *The Cosby Show*, *The Equalizer*, *A Man Called Hawk*, and an ABC Afterschool Special titled *The Gift of Amazing Grace* with Tempestt Bledsoe and Della Reese.
1988	Makes first film *Fall from Grace*, a short documentary about homelessness, while attending The New School.
1988	Acting role (as "Perry") in filmmaker Spike Lee's second theatrical feature film, *School Daze*, with Laurence Fishburne, Giancarlo Esposito, Tisha Campbell, and Samuel Jackson (Jackson later stars in Lemmons's first two feature films, *Eve's Bayou* and *The Caveman's Valentine*).
1988	First starring role in a feature film: *Vampire's Kiss* (as "Jackie") with Nicholas Cage.
1989–90	Acting roles in television movies *The Court-Martial of Jackie Robinson* (as "Rachel") and *The Great Los Angeles Earthquake* (as "Melanie Bryant"), and the soap opera *Another World*.

1991	Acting role in Jonathan Demme's *Silence of the Lambs* (as "Ardelia Mapp") with Jodie Foster and Anthony Hopkins. The film won five Academy Awards: Best Picture, Best Director, Best Actor, Best Actress, and Best Adapted Screenplay.
1991	Acting role (as "Cookie") in Robert Townsend's theatrical feature film *The Five Heartbeats* with Diahann Carroll (who later starred in Lemmons's first feature film, *Eve's Bayou*).
1991–95	Acting roles in television movies *Before the Storm* (1991), *Afterburn* (1992), and *Zooman* (1995), and in the television series *Under Cover*, *Murder, She Wrote*, and *Walker, Texas Ranger*.
1992	Starring role in Bernard Rose's theatrical feature *Candyman* (as "Bernadette Walsh").
1993	Stars in John Woo's theatrical film *Hard Target* (as "May Mitchell") with Jean-Claude van Damme, Lance Henriksen, and Wilford Brimley.
1993	Stars in Rusty Cundieff's film *Fear of a Black Hat*, which premiered at Sundance in 1993 and released in theaters in 1994.
1994	Stars in the feature film *D.R.O.P. Squad* with Eriq La Salle, Ving Rhames, and Vondie Curtis-Hall. (Curtis-Hall will later star in Lemmons's films *Dr. Hugo*, *Eve's Bayou*, *Talk to Me*, and *Harriet* as well as direct the film *Gridlock'd*, in which Lemmons appears.)
1995	Marries actor/director Vondie Curtis-Hall, with whom she collaborates on several projects (see previous note).
1996	Writer and director of the short film *Dr. Hugo* (re-released in 1998), which is based on a segment of the script for *Eve's Bayou*, starring Vondie Curtis-Hall in the lead role.
1997	*Eve's Bayou*, Lemmons's feature film debut as writer and director, is released. The film stars Jurnee Smollett, Meagan Good, Samuel Jackson, Lynn Whitfield, Debbi Morgan, and Vondie Curtis-Hall. Lemmons wins several awards for *Eve's Bayou*, including the Independent Spirit Award for Best First Feature and the Outstanding Directorial Debut award from the National Board of Review.
1997	Film role (as "Madonna") in Vondie Curtis-Hall's feature *Gridlock'd*, which also features Lemmons's and Curtis-Hall's son, Henry Hunter Hall, in his first film role.
1997	Role (as "Angenelle") in the feature film *'Til There Was You*, directed by Scott Winant and starring Jeanne Tripplehorn and Dylan McDermott.
1997	Stars (as "Teresa") in Brad Marshland's film *Liars' Dice*.

2001	The theatrical feature film *The Caveman's Valentine*, which Lemmons directs, is released. The film stars Samuel Jackson and is written by George Dawes Green.
2002	Role in the Emmy and Golden Globe Award winning television series, *ER*.
2004	Appears in the documentary film *In the Company of Women*, a film about women in independent film, in which she is interviewed.
2006	Film role (as "Angry Black Woman") in Vondie Curtis-Hall's feature *Waist Deep* (which also stars Lemmons's son, Henry Hunter Hall).
2007	*Talk to Me* is released, a theatrical feature film directed by Lemmons and written by Michael Genet and Rick Famuyiwa. Lemmons wins the African American Film Critics Association award for Best Director and the NAACP Image Award for Outstanding Directing in a Motion Picture for the film.
2008	Vassar College's Artist in Residence.
2010–11	UCLA Regents' Lecturer in the School of Theater, Film & Television.
2012	Film role (as "Roberta Washington") in Henry-Alex Rubin's theatrical feature *Disconnect*.
2013	*Black Nativity* is released, a musical feature film written and directed by Lemmons, which is based on the Langston Hughes play of the same name.
2013	Begins as Associate Arts Professor at NYU's Tish School of the Arts.
2016	Artistic Director for the Sundance Institute's Screenwriter's Lab.
2016	Announcement that Lemmons will direct and executive produce a series about Madam C. J. Walker, starring Octavia Spencer, based on the biography *On Her Own Ground* (the series is later titled *Self Made: Inspired by the Life of Madam C. J. Walker*).
2017	Updated announcement that the Madam C. J. Walker mini-series will be released on Netflix in 2020 and Lemmons will be an executive producer and will direct part of the mini-series.
2017	Directs an episode of filmmaker Gina Prince-Bythewood's television series, *Shots Fired*, starring Sanaa Lathan.
2018	*Eve's Bayou* is added to The Library of Congress's National Film Registry as a culturally, historically, or aesthetically significant film.
2018	Directs an episode of Cheo Hodari Coker's Netflix series *Luke Cage*.
2018	Executive producer for short film, *Beauty*, written and directed by Joyce Sherrí.
2019	*Harriet*, directed and cowritten (with Gregory Allen Howard) by Lemmons, is released, which is the first theatrical feature film based

on the life of Harriet Tubman. The film stars Cynthia Erivo, Leslie Odom Jr., Joe Alwyn, and Janelle Monáe, as well as her husband, Vondie Curtis-Hall, and son, Henry Hunter Hall.

Filmography

Note: A partial list of Lemmons's television acting and directing work can be found in the Chronology.

SCHOOL DAZE (1988)
Producer: Spike Lee
Executive Producer: Grace Blake
Director: Spike Lee
Screenplay: Spike Lee
Cinematography: Ernest Dickerson
Production Design: Wynn Thomas
Editing: Barry Alexander Brown
Music: Bill Lee
Cast: Larry Fishburne (Dap Dunlap), Giancarlo Esposito (Julian "Big Brother Almighty" Eaves), Tisha Campbell (Jane Toussaint), Kyme (Rachel Meadows), Joe Seneca (President McPherson), Ellen Holly (Odrie McPherson), Art Evans (Cedar Cloud), Ossie Davis (Coach Odom), Bill Nunn (Da Fella Grady), James Bond III (Da Fella Monroe), Branford Marsalis (Da Fella Jordan), Kadeem Hardison (Da Fella Edge), Eric Payne (Booker T.), Spike Lee (Darrell "Half-Pint" Dunlap), Anthony Thompkins (Doo-Doo Breath), Darryl M. Bell (Big Brother X-Ray Vision), Joie Lee (Lizzie Life), Alva Rogers (Doris Witherspoon), Paula Brown (Miriam), Jasmine Guy (Dina), Samuel L. Jackson (Leeds), Roger Guenveur Smith (Yoda), Dominic Hoffman (Mustafa), Cinqué Lee (Buckwheat), **Kasi Lemmons** (Perry)
121 minutes

VAMPIRE'S KISS (1988)
Producers: John Daly, Derek Gibson, Barry Shils, Barbara Zitwer
Director: Robert Bierman
Screenplay: Joseph Minion
Cinematography: Stefan Czapsky
Production Design: Christopher Nowak
Editing: Angus Newton
Music: Colin Towns

Cast: Nicolas Cage (Peter Loew), María Conchita Alonso (Alva Restrepo), Jennifer Beals (Rachel), Elizabeth Ashley (Dr. Glaser), **Kasi Lemmons** (Jackie), Bob Lujan (Emilio Restrepo), Jessica Lundy (Sharon), John Walker (Donald), Boris Leskin (Fantasy Cabbie), Michael Knowles (Andrew), John Michael Higgins (Ed), Jodie Markell (Joke Girl), Marc Coppola (Joke Guy), David Pierce (Theater Guy), Amy Stiller (Theater Girl)

103 minutes

THE SILENCE OF THE LAMBS (1991)
Producers: Ron Bozman, Edward Saxon, Kenneth Utt
Executive Producer: Gary Goetzman
Director: Jonathan Demme
Screenplay: Ted Tally
Cinematography: Tak Fujimoto
Production Design: Kristi Zea
Editing: Craig McKay
Music: Howard Shore
Cast: Jodie Foster (Clarice Starling), Masha Skorobogatov (young Clarice), Anthony Hopkins (Dr. Hannibal Lecter), Scott Glenn (Jack Crawford), Ted Levine (Jame "Buffalo Bill" Gumb), Anthony Heald (Frederick Chilton), Brooke Smith (Catherine Martin), Diane Baker (US Senator Ruth Martin), **Kasi Lemmons** (Ardelia Mapp), Frankie Faison (Barney Matthews), Tracey Walter (Lamar), Charles Napier (Lt. Boyle), Danny Darst (Sgt. Tate), Alex Coleman (Sgt. Jim Pembry), Dan Butler (Roden), Paul Lazar (Pilcher), Ron Vawter (Paul Krendler), Roger Corman (FBI Director Hayden Burke), Chris Isaak (SWAT Commander), Harry Northup (Mr. Bimmel), Brent Hinkley (Officer Murray)

118 minutes

THE FIVE HEARTBEATS (1991)
Producers: Loretha C. Jones, Robert Townsend
Director: Robert Townsend
Screenplay: Robert Townsend, Keenen Ivory Wayans
Cinematography: Bill Dill
Art Direction: Don Diers
Production Design: Wynn Thomas
Editing: John Carter
Music: Stanley Clarke
Cast: Robert Townsend (Duck), Michael Wright (Eddie), Leon (J. T.)
Harry Lennix (Dresser), Tico Wells (Choirboy), Diahann Carroll (Eleanor Potter), Harold Nicholas (Sarge), Tressa Thomas (Duck's Baby Sister), John Canada

Terrell (Michael 'Flash' Turner), Chuck Patterson (Jimmy Potter), Hawthorne James (Big Red), Roy Fegan (Bird), Troy Byer (Baby Doll), Carla Brothers (Tanya Sawyer), Deborah Lacey (Rose) Theresa Randle (Brenda), John Witherspoon (Wild Rudy), Anne-Marie Johnson (Sydney Todd), Lisa Mende (Marcia Sayles), Bobby McGee (Leon), Don Barnes (Lester), O.L. Duke (Monroe), Lamont Johnson (Bobby Cassanova), Arnold Johnson (Mr. Matthews), Veronica Redd (Mrs. Matthews), David McKnight (Pastor Stone), Phyllis, Applegate (Myra Stone), Paul Benjamin (Mr. King), Marilyn Coleman (Mrs. King), Norma Donaldson (Mrs. Sawyer), Harris Peet (Phil Shumway), **Kasi Lemmons** (Cookie), Monique Mannen (Sandra Tillman)
122 minutes

CANDYMAN (1992)
Producers: Steve Golin, Alan Poul, Sigurjon Sighvatsson
Executive Producer: Clive Barker
Director: Bernard Rose
Screenplay: Bernard Rose
Cinematography: Anthony B. Richmond
Production Design: Jane Ann Stewart
Editing: Dan Rae
Music: Philip Glass
Cast: Virginia Madsen (Helen Lyle), Tony Todd (Candyman), Xander Berkeley (Trevor Lyle), Vanessa A. Williams (Anne-Marie McCoy), **Kasi Lemmons** (Bernadette "Bernie" Walsh), DeJuan Guy (Jake), Gilbert Lewis (Detective Frank Valento), Carolyn Lowery (Stacey), Stanley DeSantis (Dr. Burke), Ted Raimi (Billy), Michael Culkin (Phillip Purcell), Bernard Rose (Archie Walsh), Eric Edwards (Harold), Rusty Schwimmer (Policewoman)
101 minutes

FEAR OF A BLACK HAT (1993)
Producer: Darin Scott
Executive Producer: W. M. Christopher Gorog
Director: Rusty Cundieff
Screenplay: Rusty Cundieff
Cinematography: John Demps Jr.
Production Design: Stuart Blatt
Editing: Karen Horn
Composer: Jim Manzie
Music Supervisor: Larry Robinson

Cast: Mark Christopher Lawrence (Tone Def), Larry B. Scott (Tasty Taste), Rusty Cundieff (Ice Cold), **Kasi Lemmons** (Nina Blackburn), Howie Gold (Guy Friesch), G. Smokey Campbell (Backstage Manager), Bobby Mardis (Promoter), Brad Sanders (Promoter), Moon Jones (Jam Boy), Tim Hutchinson (Reggie Clay), Faizon Love (Jam Boy), Deezer D (Jam Boy), Darin Scott (Security Head), Devin Kamin (Vanilla Sherbet), Jeff Burr (Chicago Cop), Kenneth J. Hall (John Liggert), Don Reed (Daryll in Charge), Reggie Bruce (Video Director), Barry Shabaka Henley (Geoffrey Lennox), Kurt Loder (Kurt Loder), Mark Selinger (Right Winger), Lamont Johnson (MC Slammer)
88 minutes

HARD TARGET (1993)
Producers: Sean Daniel, James Jacks
Executive Producers: Moshe Diamant, Sam Raimi, Rob Tapert
Director: John Woo
Screenplay: Chuck Pfarrer
Cinematography: Russell Carpenter
Production Design: Phil Dagort
Editing: Bob Murawski
Music: Graeme Revell, Tim Simonec
Cast: Chuck Pfarrer (Douglas Binder), Robert Apisa (Mr. Lopacki), Arnold Vosloo (Pik van Cleef), Lance Henriksen (Emil Fouchon), Douglas Rye (Frick), Mike Leinert (Frack) Yancy Butler (Natasha 'Nat' Binder), Lenore Banks (Marie), Willie C. Carpenter (Elijah Roper), Jean-Claude Van Damme (Chance Boudreaux), Barbara Tasker (Waitress), **Kasi Lemmons** (Det. Marie Mitchell), Randy Cheramie (Shop Steward), Eliott Keener (Randal Poe), Robert Pavlovich (Detective), Marco St. John (Dr. Morton), Joe Warfield (Ismal Zenan), Jeanette Kontomitras (Madam), Ted Raimi (Man on the Street), Sven-Ole Thorsen (Stephan), Tom Lupo (Jerome), Jules Sylvester (Peterson), David Efron (Billy Bob), Wilford Brimley (Uncle Douvee)
88 minutes

D.R.O.P. SQUAD (1994)
Producers: Butch Robinson, Shelby Stone
Executive Producer: Spike Lee
Director: David C. Johnson
Screenplay: David C. Johnson, Butch Robinson
Story: David Taylor, David C. Johnson, Butch Robinson
Cinematography: Ken Kelsch

Production Design: Ina Mayhew
Editing: Kevin Lee
Music: Michael Bearden
Cast: Eriq La Salle (Bruford Jamison Jr), Vondie Curtis-Hall (Rocky Seavers), Ving Rhames (Garvey), **Kasi Lemmons** (June Vanderpool), Leonard L. Thomas (XB), Nicole Powell (Lenora Jamison), Eric Payne (Stokely), Crystal Fox (Zora), Vanessa Williams (Mali), Michael Ralph (Trevor), Billy "Sly" Williams (Huey), Kim Hawthorne (Harriet), Afemo Omilami (Berl "Flip" Mangum), Spike Lee (Himself)
86 minutes

DR. HUGO (1996)
Producers: Caldecot Chubb, Cevin Cathell
Director: **Kasi Lemmons**
Screenplay: **Kasi Lemmons**
Cinematography: Amy Vincent
Production Design: Atli Arason
Editing: David Codron
Music: Vernon Reid
Cast: Vondie Curtis-Hall (Dr. Hugo), Michael Beach (Hobbs), Victoria Rowell (Stevie), Kelli Wheeler (Fred), Stacye Branche (Blanche)
19 minutes

EVE'S BAYOU (1997)
Producers: Caldecot Chubb, Samuel L. Jackson
Executive Producers: Mark Amin, Eli Selden, Nick Wechsler, Julie Silverman Yorn
Director: **Kasi Lemmons**
Screenplay: **Kasi Lemmons**
Cinematography: Amy Vincent
Art Direction: Adele Plauche
Production Design: Jeff Howard
Editing: Terilyn A. Shropshire
Music: Terence Blanchard
Cast: Tamara Tunie (Narrator), Jurnee Smollett (Eve Batiste), Meagan Good (Cisely Batiste), Lynn Whitfield (Roz Batiste), Samuel L. Jackson (Louis Batiste), Debbi Morgan (Mozelle Batiste), Diahann Carroll (Elzora), Jake Smollett (Poe Batiste), Ethel Ayler (Gran Mere), Vondie Curtis-Hall (Julian Grayraven), Roger Guenveur Smith (Lenny Mereaux), Lisa Nicole Carson (Matty Mereaux), Branford Marsalis (Harry), Victoria Rowell (Stevie Hobbs), Leonard L. Thomas (Maynard)
109 minutes

GRIDLOCK'D (1997)
Producers: Erica Huggins, Damian Jones, Paul Webster
Executive Producers: Ted Field, Scott Kroopf, Russell Simmons
Director: Vondie Curtis-Hall
Screenplay: Vondie Curtis-Hall
Cinematography: Bill Pope
Art Direction: Scott Plauche
Production Design: Dan Bishop
Editing: Christopher Koefoed
Music: Stewart Copeland
Cast: Tupac Shakur (Spoon), Tim Roth (Stretch), Lucy Liu (Cee-Cee), Thandie
Newton (Cookie), Charles Fleischer (Mr. Woodson), Bokeem Woodbine (Mud),
Howard Hesseman (Blind man), John Sayles (Cop #1), Eric Payne (Cop #2), Tom
Towles (D-Reper's Henchman), Tom Wright (Koolaid), Billie Neal (Medicaid
woman #1), James Pickens Jr. (Supervisor), Debra Wilson (Medicaid woman
#2), Rusty Schwimmer (Medicaid nurse), Richmond Arquette (Resident doc-
tor), Elizabeth Peña (Admissions person), **Kasi Lemmons** (Madonna), Vondie
Curtis-Hall (D-Reper)
91 minutes

'TIL THERE WAS YOU (1997)
Producers: Penney Finkelman Cox, Alan Poul, Tom Rosenberg
Executive Producers: Sigurjon Sighvatsson, Ted Tannebaum
Director: Scott Winant
Screenplay: Winnie Holzman
Cinematography: Bobby Bukowski
Art Direction: Randy Moore
Production Design: Craig Stearns
Editing: Joanna Cappuccilli, Richard Marks
Music: Terence Blanchard, Miles Goodman
Cast: Jeanne Tripplehorn (Gwen Moss), Yvonne Zima (Gwen, age 7), Madeline
Zima (Gwen, age 12), Dylan McDermott (Nick Dawkan), Kellen Fink (Nick,
age 7), Joshua Rubin (Nick, age 12), Sarah Jessica Parker (Francesca Lanfield),
Jennifer Aniston (Debbie), Amanda Fuller (Debbie, age 13), Craig Bierko (Jon
Haas), Christine Ebersole (Beebee Moss), Janel Moloney (Beebee, age 25), Michael
Tucker (Saul Moss), John Plumpis (Saul Moss, age 25), Michael Moertl (Dean),
Karen Allen (Betty Dawkan), Kale Browne (Vince Dawkan), Alice Drummond
(Harriet), Ken Olin (Gregory), Patrick Malahide (Timo), Nina Foch (Sophia
Monroe), Reg Rogers (Bob), Susan Walters (Robin), **Kasi Lemmons** (Angenelle),

Steve Antin as Kevin Richard Fancy (Murdstone), Earl Carroll (Heep), Ian Gomez (Scott)
113 minutes

LIARS' DICE (1997)
Producers: Yule Caise, Brad Marshland
Executive Producers: Jonathan Askin
Director: Brad Marshland
Screenplay: Brad Marshland
Production Design: Jonathan Wornick
Editing: Philip Steinman
Music: Jim Latham
Cast: Yule Caise (Boyden), Kawena Charlot (Lynette), **Kasi Lemmons** (Teresa), Dean Norris (Hodge), Tricia Stewart (Claire)
78 minutes

THE CAVEMAN'S VALETINE (2001)
Producers: Danny DeVito, Scott Frank, Elie Samaha, Michael Shamberg, Stacey Sher, Andrew Stevens
Executive Producers: Nicolas Clermont, Samuel L. Jackson, Eli Selden, Julie Yorn
Director: **Kasi Lemmons**
Screenplay: George Dawes Green
Cinematography: Amy Vincent
Art Direction: Grant Van Der Slagt
Production Design: Robin Standefer
Editing: Terilyn A. Shropshire
Music: Terence Blanchard
Cast: Samuel L. Jackson (Romulus Ledbetter), Colm Feore (David Leppenraub), Aunjanue Ellis (Officer Lulu Ledbetter), Tamara Tunie (Sheila Ledbetter), Jay Rodan (Joey Peasley), Ann Magnuson (Moira Leppenraub), Anthony Michael Hall (Bob), Sean Macmahon (Scotty Gates), Jeff Geddis (Paul)
105 minutes

WAIST DEEP (2006)
Producer: Preston L. Holmes
Executive Producers: A. Demetrius Brown, Marc D. Evans, Ted Field, Amy J. Kaufman, Stan Lathan, Trevor Macy, Delaney McGill, Russell Simmons
Director: Vondie Curtis-Hall
Screenplay: Vondie Curtis-Hall, Darin Scott
Story: Michael Mahern

Cinematography: Shane Hurlbut
Art Direction: Yoo Jung Han
Production Design: Warren Alan Young
Editing: Terilyn A. Shropshire
Music: Terence Blanchard
Cast: Tyrese Gibson (O2), Shawn Parr (Newscaster #1), Henry Hunter Hall (Junior), Johnny C. Pruitt (Guard), Meagan Good (Coco), Darris Love (Rock), Larenz Tate (Lucky), William Duffy (Newscaster #2), Game (Meat), Kimora Lee Simmons (Fencing House Lady), DeWayne Turrentine Jr. (Gangster #1), Paul Terrell Clayton (Black Security Guard), Ray Bengston (White Security Guard), Earl Minfield (Bank Manager), Dagmar Stansova (Bank Woman), **Kasi Lemmons** (Angry Black Woman), Laura Miro (Newscaster #3), Thommy Abate (Look-A-Like), Dawn Reavis (Newscaster #4), Dylan Tays (Newscaster #5)
97 minutes

TALK TO ME (2007)
Producers: Joe Fries, Mark Gordon, Sidney Kimmel, Josh McLaughlin
Executive Producers: Don Cheadle, J. Miles Dale, William Horberg, Joey Rappa, Bruce Toll
Director: **Kasi Lemmons**
Screenplay: Michael Genet, Rick Famuyiwa
Cinematography: Stéphane Fontaine
Art Direction: Patrick Banister
Production Design: Warren Alan Young
Editing: Terilyn A. Shropshire
Music: Terence Blanchard
Cast: Don Cheadle (Ralph "Petey" Greene), Chiwetel Ejiofor (Dewey Hughes), Taraji P. Henson (Vernell Watson), Cedric the Entertainer ("Nighthawk" Bob Terry), Mike Epps (Milo Hughes), Martin Sheen (E.G. Sonderling), Vondie Curtis-Hall (Sunny Jim Kelsey), Richard Chevolleau (Poochie Braxton), Alison Sealy-Smith (Freda), Elle Downs (Peaches), Herbert L. Rawlings Jr. (James Brown), Damir Andrei (Frederick de Cordova), Jim Malmberg (Johnny Carson)
118 minutes

DISCONNECT (2012)
Producers: William Horberg, Mickey Liddell, Jennifer Monroe
Executive Producers: Scott Ferguson, Marc Forster, Brad Simpson
Director: Henry Alex Rubin
Screenplay: Andrew Stern
Cinematography: Ken Seng

Art Direction: Jennifer Dehghan
Production Design: Dina Goldman
Editing: Lee Percy, Kevin Tent
Music: Max Richter
Cast: Jason Bateman (Rich Boyd), Hope Davis (Lydia Boyd), Frank Grillo (Mike Dixon), Paula Patton (Cindy Hull), Andrea Riseborough (Nina Dunham), Tessa Albertson (Isabella), Alexander Skarsgård (Derek Hull), Michael Nyqvist (Stephen Schumacher), Max Thieriot (Kyle), Marc Jacobs (Harvey), Colin Ford (Jason Dixon), Jonah Bobo (Ben Boyd), Haley Ramm (Abby Boyd), Norbert Leo Butz (Peter), **Kasi Lemmons** (Roberta Washington), John Sharian (Ross Lynd), Aviad Bernstein (Frye)
115 minutes

BLACK NATIVITY (2013)
Producers: William Horberg, T.D. Jakes, Galt Niederhoffer, Celine Rattray
Executive Producers: Joy Goodwin, Trudie Styler, Derrick Williams
Director: **Kasi Lemmons**
Screenplay: **Kasi Lemmons**
Based on the play by: Langston Hughes
Cinematography: Anastas N. Michos
Art Direction: Doug Huszti
Production Design: Kristi Zea
Editing: Terilyn A. Shropshire
Music: Laura Karpman, Raphael Saadiq
Cast: Forest Whitaker (Reverend Cornell Cobbs), Angela Bassett (Aretha Cobbs), Tyrese Gibson (Tyson/Loot), Jennifer Hudson (Naima), Mary J. Blige (Angel), Vondie Curtis-Hall (Pawnbroker), Nas (Isaiah), Jacob Latimore (Langston), Rotimi (Officer Butch McDaniels), Luke James (Jo-Jo/Joseph)
93 minutes

HARRIET (2019)
Producers: Debra Martin Chase, Gregory Allen Howard, Daniela Taplin Lundberg
Executive Producers: Nnamdi Asomugha, Bill Benenson, Pen Densham, Shea Kammer, Kristina Kendall, Charles D. King, Elizabeth Koch, John Watson
Director: **Kasi Lemmons**
Screenplay: Gregory Allen Howard, **Kasi Lemmons**
Cinematography: John Toll
Art Direction: Kevin Hardison, Christina Eunji Kim
Production Design: Warren Alan Young
Editing: Wyatt Smith

Music: Terence Blanchard

Cast: Cynthia Erivo (Harriet Tubman/Minty), Leslie Odom Jr. (William Still), Janelle Monáe (Marie Buchanon), Joe Alwyn (Gideon Brodess), Deborah Ayorinde (Rachel Ross), Vondie Curtis-Hall (Reverend Samuel Green), Jennifer Nettles (Eliza Brodess), Clarke Peters (Ben Ross), Vanessa Bell Calloway (Rit Ross), Zackary Momoh (John Tubman), Omar J. Dorsey (Bigger Long), Henry Hunter Hall (Walter)

125 minutes

Kasi Lemmons: Interviews

A Conversation with … Kasi Lemmons

Susan Bullington Katz / 1997

From *Conversations with Screenwriters* by Susan Bullington Katz. Portsmouth, NH: Heinemann.

You may recognize her as Jodie Foster's roommate in *Silence of the Lambs* or from her roles in *'Til There Was You, Gridlock'd, Fear of a Black Hat, Vampire's Kiss,* and *Hard Target,* but Kasi Lemmons has also been a member of the Writers Guild since '87, since shortly after she auditioned for *The Cosby Show* and Bill Cosby discovered she could write. Now she's written and directed her first feature, *Eve's Bayou.*

Based on a story she wrote several years ago, *Eve's Bayou* is about an African American family in Louisiana, told through the eyes of the ten-year-old daughter. And it wasn't an easy road to getting it made. What's more, when things finally fell into place, she had just had a new baby, so she shot the movie with a three-month-old in tow. Now, though, she says Hunter feels very much at home on a set, thinking it a matter of course that 150 cast and crew members would greet him with a smile every morning.

And now Kasi herself is at home in front of the computer, having written several more features since *Eve's Bayou.* From Paris, where she was working on a script with her husband, actor/writer/director Vondie Curtis-Hall, she took time out to talk about acting and writing and how it took *Waiting to Exhale* before backers finally began to acknowledge an audience for movies about African Americans that were about things other than the 'hood.

Kasi Lemmons: *Eve's Bayou* was my first full-length script that I wrote by myself. I wrote it a long time ago. And since then I got to write a few before we got to make *Eve's Bayou*, but it was the first one I wrote by myself. I had written a project for Bill Cosby with two other women—that was in '87, I think—and then afterwards I wrote a project with a friend of mine.

Susan Bullington Katz: What was the project for Bill Cosby?

Lemmons: We called it *Tight Shoes*, and I don't think they ever did anything with it. He wanted three Black women to write him a script . . . At the time I had just been writing scenes for friends of mine to do in acting class.

I was an actress first, but I always wrote. I wrote even when I was a kid.

And then around '86, I started writing short stories. And I had actually written a short story that was kind of part of *Eve's Bayou*. And I started writing these scenes for actors. The first class that I took in playwriting was John Ford Noonan's class at the "Y" in New York. That was my first formal education in dramatic writing.

And then in film school—at the New School—I made two films. One was kind of a docudrama which really broke form and broke the rules . . . Some people really loved it, it did really well, but it pissed a lot of people off because I had a voice-over over this kind of documentary.

It was called *Fall from Grace*, and it was about homeless people in New York. I didn't know that there were rules to making documentaries, so I did a whole bunch of different things. We had talked to some homeless people on the street, and I had kind of composed a voice-over that Vondie read. And we had put this rap music over it and a lot of it was long angle shots of homeless people. And it was kind of controversial because of the voice-over.

The film did really well. Comic Relief used pieces of it, and it did a bunch of festivals around the world. For a seven-minute piece, I got some mileage out of it. And every once in a while, people would come up to me and tell me they were slightly offended by it because I had put this voice-over over this kind of heartbreaking footage. . . . But we didn't know—we thought it was cool. And I still really like that film.

Then I showed that film to Bill Cosby. I went in for an audition, and I said to myself, gearing up for the audition, "You know, if I ever get to meet Mr. Cosby, I'm going to show him my film." And I don't know what I expected, but he said to me, "What I really need is a writer. Can you write?" And I said, "Yes, as a matter of fact, I write scenes for my friends." And he said, "Well, write me a scene, and bring it in next week and show it to my head writer." So I came in the next Tuesday with my scene, which was perfect, 'cause that's what I was doing, you know—writing scenes. And he'd forgotten, of course, that he had told me that. He was totally not expecting me. But he gave my scene to his head writer, Matt Robinson, who hired me as part of a team of writers to write this movie for him.

Katz: Were you on the show at that point?

Lemmons: No, I didn't get the part. But I got this writing job. And I guess it really changed my life.

Then I got *Silence of the Lambs* (as an actress), and the career was going okay. We moved to Los Angeles, and I wrote a script with a friend of mine, Billie Neal, who's also an actress and an extraordinary writer. We wrote a script together called *He Ain't Dead Yet*. And it was after that that I wrote *Eve's Bayou*.

I wrote it just for me I was going to put it in a drawer and not show it to anybody. It was very personal. It was something I needed to experiment with.

Katz: In what way?

Lemmons: Well, I thought I wanted to write a novel. And then I thought it would be fun to experiment with writing a screenplay as if it were a novel. So *Eve's Bayou* is kind of literary in a way. Then also I was experimenting with the type of prose. To me, it has a rhythm, like a long poem. So I was experimenting, and I didn't know if I was going to be good at it. It didn't occur to me to really show it to people. I showed it to Vondie when I finished it, and he loved it, and he said, "You've gotta show this to somebody." So I showed it to my acting agent—I didn't know who else to show it to! And he gave it to the literary agent at the agency where he was, and that's still my agent: Frank Wuliger. Frank Wuliger really helped me set up *Eve's Bayou*. But I truly wasn't going to show it to anybody.

Katz: When you say it had a rhythm to it as you were writing it, were you fitting it into this rhythm?

Lemmons: I didn't even try to make it fit into the rhythm. It naturally came out that way. But it was an experiment. I haven't really done the same thing since. I write poetry, really bad poetry—my mom writes great poetry—but it's almost like when you write poetry, you have a poem that kind of builds up inside you and then you have to spit it out, right? *Eve's Bayou* was a little bit like that. Like it built up inside of me and it just came out in a certain rhythm.

In a way, it's almost like now I would be more embarrassed to do it, because it was another time in my life when I wasn't concerned with the rules at all. Now that I'm kind of a professional screenwriter, I wonder if I might have been more self-conscious . . . But I felt definitely liberated by the fact that I wasn't planning on showing it to anybody. I didn't care if anybody liked it. It made me laugh and cry. And I would sit there and cry and laugh, and that was really what I needed to get out of it, and I didn't really need anything else. All the rest has been icing.

Katz: You mentioned that it's personal. Were parts of it autobiographical?

Lemmons: No, none of it is autobiographical. That's not really what I mean by personal. I guess it was a way of talking about a family. You know, I think that any writer who writes anything about a family, whether a novelist or a playwright, there are some of their family that are going to sneak in it, right? Or their best friend's family, or families that they've known, their cousin's family. So there are definitely parts of my family in it, but it's not at all autobiographical.

Katz: I don't know the Creole life, but this movie sure seems to be Creole life in all caps. How much of that world did you know about before writing it?

Lemmons: I think I knew about it—it sounds goofy, but—in some sort of spiritual way. Because in fact I made it up. I was trying to have a story take place with all Black characters and kind of liberate them to have made their own kind of town. That they were absolutely indigenous to this place where they owned the world. And they weren't necessarily feeling the weight of white oppression. Not that I'm not interested in that story, but it wasn't what this particular story was about. And I wanted them to be kings and queens in this. I knew there were places in Louisiana where the culture hadn't changed, or had changed in its own kind of interesting way, but places that had their own rules. So Eve's Bayou, I just made up this town that had its own rules and its own specific history, and that they were Creole.

And then late in the film, in preproduction; I sought out a Creole consultant—somebody who actually speaks the language, because it's a kind of lost language . . . But you know what was interesting?

Katz: What's that?

Lemmons: In preproduction I bought a book—I bought a lot of books for research—and I wish I could remember the exact title, but it was called something like *The Lost Negro People of the Cane River*. It's a history book. And in this book they describe this little town, right, up in the Cane River? And they tell this story that happened. This woman, I think her name was Maria Theresa, had a slave. And she became very sick with, like, cholera. And the slave woman saved her with a type of magic medicine. And the woman gave her the town. Or gave her some huge piece of property, which is exactly how Eve's Bayou gets started in my story.

So it was really weird. That's why I say, even though it might sound goofy, I think I kind of knew about it on some spiritual level that a place like this could exist.

Katz: That's always fascinating to read something like that after the fact.

Lemmons: It was really weird. It was my production designer, we were sitting in the van on the location scout, and he started reading me this paragraph, and we all turned around, and it was hard for everybody to believe for a second that I hadn't read the book before, but I hadn't. I don't even think you can buy it outside of Louisiana. And it was just very, very interesting. Of course, that's my little history of Eve's Bayou. Jean Paul Batiste was stricken with cholera and the slave woman saves his life and he gives her that piece of land. And of course they begat the entire town.

Katz: How did you end up directing this film? You didn't start out directing it, right?

Lemmons: I think originally I wanted to be in it. And then when people started really liking it . . . Oh, maybe somebody can actually direct this movie soon, you know, and my movie can get made! And that was pretty darned appealing. Then when that started getting more serious, I literally woke up one day on my birthday—I had already formed a partnership with Cotty (Chubb)— and I woke up on my birthday and I said, "I'm directing that movie." At the time we were talking about some very good directors whom I entirely respect, but I don't know, I woke up one day on my birthday and I wanted it. And I didn't want anybody else to have it. And I called my agent and I said, "I've had an epiphany and I must direct this—" And he's like, "Okay, okay, wait a minute." 'Cause we were already talking to all these people. . . .

Katz: You mean all these other directors who were thinking about it?

Lemmons: Yeah. And it was the best birthday present I've ever given myself. I wanted it, and I didn't want anybody else to do it . . . And when Cotty and my agent finally got over the shock that I had made this announcement that I was going to direct it, they took it very seriously. And Cotty said, "Okay, well, if that's the case, then we need to do a short, because I'm not doing a feature with you if you've never directed anything." I mean, I had made little documentaries in film school, but that wasn't going to get it, you know. So we made the short together—I think he was probably seeing if he thought I was a director at all and to have something to show people. But they supported me instantly. As soon as they got over the shock, they were totally supportive, and they always have been.

Katz: Tell me about the short. How short was it?

Lemmons: The short is about twenty minutes long. It was a scene that I had cut out of *Eve's Bayou*. It kind of got back in later on, something kind of similar to it.

Katz: Which scene was it?

Lemmons: There's a section of the film where Sam goes doctoring, and he has the little girl with him. And he goes and visits a lady, a beautiful sexy lady, (played by) Victoria Rowell. It's kind of that. That scene. But not exactly. Very inexactly. Inspired by that. It's just this little tiny, tiny piece and I made it into a full little film that has its own beginning and its own end, where a doctor pays a visit to a married lady.

Katz: Who did you use for your actors?

Lemmons: I used my husband conveniently to play the lead. It's like, who can you get for free on Memorial Day weekend to act in your short? I happen to have extremely talented friends, so I'm really really lucky. Victoria flew back from France to do it. And Mike Beach, who's another friend of mine who's extraordinary. And this magnificent little girl named Kelli Wheeler.

Katz: You shot it over a weekend?

Lemmons: We shot it over four days. We started on Thursday or Friday and we went until Monday. My agents lent me half the money.

Katz: That was my next question.

Lemmons: And Cotty Chubb put up the other half like out of his bank account—so it was one of those labors of love. I mean, when I say I got support, I really got support.

Katz: That sure is. I know of Cotty from IFP (Independent Feature Project) West. How did he get hold of *Eve's Bayou* in the first place?

Lemmons: Frank had sent the script to several people, and I had taken a lot of meetings. And one day he called me up and he said, "I've got this guy that I want you to meet. He's eccentric," he said, "but he's the man who can get your movie made." And I met him, and he was very passionate about the script, and he seemed to mean what he said and, in fact, he did.

Katz: In what ways?

Lemmons: You know, a lot of people were interested in this script as a writing sample. They thought, "Oh, this is a really fascinating writing sample, but what I really would like is for you to write a script about *this*"—you know what I mean? But Cotty really wanted to make *Eve's Bayou*.

Eve's Bayou is one of these scripts that had a lot of fans, but people weren't just jumping over each other to make it. They thought it would be a difficult film to make.

Katz: Why did they think it would be difficult?

Lemmons: An all African American cast was the major reason. To make a small film that didn't have a lot of violence, that wasn't a street kind of "in the hood" movie with an all-African American cast—kind of a new concept.

Katz: Pretty amazing, isn't it?

Lemmons: It's amazing. But remember those articles about where everybody was surprised that there was a *Waiting to Exhale* audience? We're talking about an audience that people didn't know existed until *Waiting to Exhale*. Which is a shame, but true. So from where they were looking at my script, here is something that we all admire, but we can't figure out who is going to see this movie. So it was difficult for them.

Katz: How was Cotty different about that?

Lemmons: Cotty saw it as a piece of art. He could isolate it. He could look at it and say, "I really like this, and I think this is worth making." I mean, he'd be the first person to tell you he wouldn't want to take a movie that nobody wants to see. But on the other hand, I think he's an idealist. He sees things as, "This is something I would really like to see made." And I needed that, you know. We all do. I don't believe it would have gotten made without him.

Katz: That's great. It seems like you have a whole huge slate of projects you're working on or have been working on or have finished. Are these from people having seen or read *Eve's Bayou*?

Lemmons: Yeah. Everything I got is pretty much because people saw or read *Eve's Bayou*. Right after I made *Eve's Bayou*, some of the first people that saw it were Michelle Pfeiffer and Kate Guinzburg, and kind of bravely, I think, they had me in for a meeting with Kate Guinzburg, and she asked me to write a script for Michelle Pfeiffer. I wrote a script called *Privacy* that everybody seems to like a good deal. It's totally diametrically opposed to *Eve's Bayou*. It couldn't be more opposite.

Katz: How so?

Lemmons: Well, it's all white. And it's edgy, in a way. *Eve's Bayou* is kind of lyrical and slow, and *Privacy* is edgier. It has a different pace. It has a whole different rhythm. I love them both.

And I wrote a piece for Whitney Houston called *Eight Pieces for Josette* for Warner Brothers that we're hoping to do at some point. That's something else that I'm really proud of. It's about the classical music world.

And I wrote a movie for Cotty, actually, that I like very much, too. And now I'm writing a movie with my husband.

Katz: What is the movie you're writing with Vondie?

Lemmons: It's for him to direct, and it's an adaptation of a book, called *The Impersonator*, by Diane Hammond.

Katz: When you actually sat down and started writing, how do you think your acting background influenced your writing?

Lemmons: I wrote things that I wanted to say. When I wrote *Eve's Bayou*, I played all of the parts. And I wrote things that I as an actor would have loved to say. You know, "I'd love to have this monologue." "I'd love to say this line." And I think that acting and writing together . . . the natural marriage of that is directing.

Katz: What for you is the hardest part of writing?
Lemmons: The solitude. I get lonely sometimes.

Katz: I understand this totally.
Lemmons: Yeah. That's probably the hardest part. And then giving it over. You know, being a studio screenwriter and having to give it over. As a matter of fact, that's absolutely the hardest part. Solitude's nothing compared to that! Giving it over and letting other people give you notes on it. And they start telling you what they think the character would say or wouldn't say, and it's like, "You don't know, sonny! I made her up. How do you know what she would say?"

Katz: And have you gotten that so far?
Lemmons: Oh, of course. I mean, it's a natural part of the process. Actually, it's an important part of the process. The mature part of me knows this. It's an important part of the process because making movies is a collaboration and it's absolutely necessary to get the feedback from people who are going to put a lot of work and money into getting the movie onto the screen. And so I appreciate the process, but I find it painful. And I'm sure it's the same with all writers. I don't think I have a unique position here.

Katz: Right. But how have you figured out at this point how best to handle those meetings, where someone is telling you something that you don't necessarily think is the best way to go with it?
Lemmons: Wow. That's a difficult question. I try and talk them into seeing it my way. But if they're insistent, I try to make it work. I try to find a way of thinking about it so that it works. Or you try it, and you give it your best shot but maybe it doesn't work and then you go back to something that you suspect might work better. But I try to give it my best shot. Say, "Okay, well, I don't agree, but maybe." And I think that the best producers I've worked with look at it as a collaboration with the writer, as well.

And they appreciate my point of view so that we can negotiate. And say, "Okay, well, you give a little, I'll give a little, and we'll come up with this, and maybe this will work for all of us."

Kasi Lemmons:
The Woman behind *Eve's Bayou*

Erika Muhammad / 1998

From *Ms.*, vol. 8, no. 5 (March/April 1998), pp. 74–75. Reprinted by permission.

Writer-actor-director Kasi Lemmons's *Eve's Bayou* is somewhat of an anomaly in Hollywood—the narrative is told from the point of view of a child, the movie has an all African American cast, it's a period piece, and it has a rural setting—and Lemmons is one of only a few Black female directors who have achieved success with a mainstream release. Critics are praising this "haunting Southern Gothic" of Black Creole life in the 1960s. They applaud its deftly written script, which, set within the lush surroundings of the Louisiana bayous, tells a searing, bittersweet story of family trauma.

The film's mysticism has been compared to that evoked in the writings of Toni Morrison, Zora Neale Hurston, and Gabriel García Márquez. And Lemmons's directing has been compared to that of Ingmar Bergman. After receiving standing ovations at the Telluride and Toronto film festivals, *Eve's Bayou* became one of the highest grossing independent films of 1997, and the National Board of Review awarded Lemmons a Director's Debut Award.

What happens to a family when the boundaries that protect and define our relationships are violated? What is the price of knowledge? These questions haunt *Eve's Bayou*. They are the questions that ten-year-old Eve Batiste, the film's protagonist, struggles with—in a stunning performance by Jurnee Smollett—during one ruinous summer when her family's stability and her childhood are lost. The Batistes seem to have a perfect life: the father (Samuel L. Jackson) is a successful doctor admired by all and adored by his beautiful wife (Lynn Whitfield). Their daughters, Cisely, who's turning fourteen, and her younger sister, Eve, vie with each other and their mother for the father's attention. But the mirror cracks and adultery, alcoholism, mental abuse, and the specter of incest bubble to the surface.

Lemmons, a talented actor with a number of film credits, is currently collaborating on a script with her husband, actor-writer Vondie Curtis-Hall, who is in *Eve's Bayou.*

Erika Muhammad: What led you to this film?
Kasi Lemmons: I went to film school before my acting career developed. I made a film that I was very, very proud of called *Fall from Grace,* a little documentary about homeless people in New York City. But right after film school my acting career took off and I moved out to L.A.

As an actress I couldn't empty my soul because the parts I was playing would not allow that sense of artistic relief: Black Girl Best Friend, Black Girl Next Door, Black Girl Cop. I was frustrated and I had this story inside me. My therapist told me to take off pilot season, unplug the phone, and write my story. Pilot season is very important to an actor. You're hoping that you'll get a job and be on TV and somebody will notice you. I'd landed a pilot every season, so it was important to me financially. But it was the best advice I've ever gotten.

It took about three months and I cried the whole time. When I finished, I was drained and happy and thought that I could put the script into a drawer and never show it to anybody.

EM: What took it out of the drawer?
KL: My husband, who was my boyfriend at the time, convinced me to show it to somebody. When I showed it to my agent, he ran it down the hall to the literary agent. Frank (Wuliger), who's now my literary agent, became a fan of the project and introduced me to the producer, Cotty (Caldecot) Chubb.

EM: When did you decide to direct?
KL: We were searching for directors. I'd had meetings where people were saying things about the story that scared me. The movie's about subtlety. I didn't want to hit audiences over the head. One day—it was my birthday—I had an epiphany. I woke up and I thought, "Somebody else is going to fuck it up." So I decided that I was the person to deliver the film.

Cotty agreed to produce a short drama based on one of the scenes to see if I had any talent. What happened next? Well, with the script and the short film and me attached as director, everybody in town turned us down! I'm not bitter about this, because that's the process; they turn down everything.

EM: What was the turning point?
KL: Samuel Jackson read the script and saw the short. Sam was willing to take the

chance because he is a very adventurous actor. It was with his support (Jackson was also a producer) that it got made.

EM: You were nine months pregnant when Trimark gave the film a green light. Did you consider postponing?
KL: You know when people say that you have to be in the right place at the right time? I was ready. I was not going to say, "Oh, I'm sorry, I can't do it right now because I'm having a baby."

EM: How do you feel about the response to your film?
KL: I feel very fortunate. On the other hand, you're always trying to break the perception that you're just a Black filmmaker. Obviously, I love that and I want to be counted as an African American director. But my objective is for people to look at my movie as a work of art first. It has an all African American cast and it's an African American story. That's incredibly important and also incredibly incidental. It could be anybody's family.

EM: People ask if *Eve's Bayou* is autobiographical or based on a true story.
KL: I made this up. I like to think of it as my great fiction.

EM: What were you trying to achieve with the bayou setting?
KL: The bayou is a character in the movie. It is dark, secret, painfully beautiful. We found a place where the Batistes would have lived, and we filled the screen with water. It gives you an otherworldly, shimmering, floating feeling. It works on you in an emotional way. You're transported to another world.

EM: You raise the specter of sexual abuse and incest in the film.
KL: It's not really about incest. Certainly, a lot of that goes on and it can be a terrible, fragmenting experience for a child. What I'm talking about, which I think is infinitely more common, is inappropriate behavior between adults and children. That can also be a really hard experience for a child. It is the responsibility of the adult to create boundaries.

EM: How would you describe the character Mozelle, the two young girls' aunt?
KL: As an alternative role model. There's a stigma against women like Mozelle. Her brother, Louis (the girls' father), gets away with being extremely sexual because it's a man's world. Mozelle, who has the same sexual weakness as Louis, gets labeled as crazy. Her sexuality is perceived as dangerous because it is the 1960s and the South. And yet, Mozelle is the mirror image of her brother in a

beautiful way. Being clairvoyant, she heals the soul. As a medical doctor, Louis heals the body. In the movie, folklore is the legacy of power handed down from woman to woman.

EM: In the film, there are several rivalries among the daughters and the mother.
KL: *Eve's Bayou* is about loving so deep that it hurts, that you make mistakes. The sisters love each other, they live for each other, and they can't live without each other. It's the same with Roz, their mother, and Cisely. Roz loves Cisely, but she sees herself in her daughter. She sees this girl who's self-assured and yet fragile. Roz is a doctor's wife and that's her whole career—the beautiful children and the parties. Why does she hold on to this life even though she's disenchanted with it? She loves Louis, but he is a flawed man. You shouldn't hate Louis. You should feel compassion for him. It's easy to make everything black and white. But I am interested in the gray areas. Most people are not bad people or good people, they are in between.

Writing and Directing *Eve's Bayou*: A Talk with Kasi Lemmons

Annie Nocenti / 1998

From *Scenario: The Magazine of Screenwriting Art*, vol. 4, no. 2 (Summer 1998), pp. 192–99. Reprinted by permission.

Kasi Lemmons began her career as an actress, but always considered herself a writer. She began by writing short stories, and envisioned someday moving on to novels. Born in St. Louis, Lemmons spent her childhood shuttling between St. Louis and Tuskegee, Alabama. She studied acting at NYU's Tisch School of the Arts and history at UCLA.

Returning to New York in the early 1980s to again pursue acting, Lemmons wrote short scenes for actor friends to use as audition pieces. She took a film class at The New School where she made a short, *Fall from Grace*. On an audition in 1988 for "The Cosby Show," Lemmons asked Cosby to look at her film. He responded by wanting to know if she could write, which led to her working on the unproduced screenplay *Tight Shoes*. Lemmons continued acting, winning supporting roles in such films as *School Daze* (1988) and *Vampire's Kiss* (1989), with perhaps her most high-profile role being Jodie Foster's roommate in *The Silence of the Lambs* (1991).

Lemmons wrote the screenplay *Eve's Bayou* simply as an exercise for herself, not intending to sell or produce it. However, when her boyfriend (and future husband) Vondie Curtis-Hall, himself an actor-writer-director, read the finished script, he urged Lemmons to pursue getting it produced. She showed it to her acting agent, who in turn gave it to literary agent Frank Wuliger.

When the right director couldn't be found, Lemmons decided to direct *Eve's Bayou* herself. Producer Caldecot Chubb urged her to make a short based on a scene from the screenplay that could serve as a calling card for her skills as a director, the result being *Dr. Hugo*. When Samuel L. Jackson saw the short film and read the script, he signed on to play the leading man.

Eve's Bayou was still a tough sell—a rural period piece centered around a group of independent-minded Black women, told from a child's POV. But when the script made it into the hands of Ray Price at Trimark Pictures, the necessary funding was secured. Lemmons was nine months pregnant when her project was finally green-lit, and when she walked on-set the first day as director, she was carrying her then twelve-week-old son, Hunter.

Eve's Bayou was a rousing critical and box-office success, becoming the highest grossing independent film of 1997. It won "Best First-time Director" from the National Board of Review, the Independent Spirit Award for "Best First Feature," and received seven NAACP Image Award nominations. Lemmons is currently adapting, with Curtis-Hall, Diane Hammond's novel *The Impersonator*, to be directed by Curtis-Hall. Lemmons hopes to begin production soon on an adaptation of George Dawes Green's novel *The Caveman's Valentine*, coadapted by Lemmons and Green, directed by Lemmons, and produced by Jersey Films and Samuel L. Jackson, who will also star, thus reuniting part of the *Eve's Bayou* team.

Q: You've said that you wrote *Eve's Bayou* as "an experiment in writing a screenplay as if it were a novel."
A: As an experiment with the form. It was an experiment in creating a form. I'd written screenplays before, and I knew how to write them, but I guess I'm very much a frustrated novelist. *Eve's Bayou* had the feeling of a hybrid of a novel and a screenplay. The dialogue is very operatic, it has a certain rhythm, it's heightened, it sounds like poetry to me. It's very poetic, the descriptions are very lyrical, and that was a conscious experiment.

Q: It reads like a poetic memoir, and the narrative is layered in a novelistic way— there's the unfolding drama, and then there's the almost uber-reality of fate, voodoo, and the bayou's sense of justice. Was that also a conscious choice, or was it more intuitive?
A: I knew from the beginning, and by that I mean the conception, that I was trying to tell a story on two different levels. I wanted you to watch the movie, and depending on your belief system, view it one way or the other. To a certain extent, I was very successful with that. People will say to me: "It gives me the creeps the way that little girl killed her father with voodoo." And I think, wow! People argue with me about it. They'll say, "Well, if it wasn't voodoo, then why did Louis say that last 'Night, Matty'?"

Q: I saw it as part of Louis's character. Pride is his Achilles' heel.
A: It's hard for me to decide, because I believe *Eve's Bayou* on a lot of levels. I believe it was his pride, I think maybe it was a touch suicidal. People have suicidal

flashes all the time. Louis' life is out of control. He's walking on the edge, and that's one of those on-the-edge moments. What made him say it?

Q: Sheer orneriness!

A: Yeah! (laughs) But the questions in *Eve's Bayou* are more interesting to me than the answers.

Q: Roz comes from the character lineage of Louis' mother, Beatrice, and silent suffering. Roz has a bit of the Cinderella syndrome—just wait it out, like the fortune-teller advises.

A: She is very much, and intentionally, a long-suffering wife. Her position as a doctor's wife, and as woman of the house, is very important to her. She is a Jackie Kennedy. She is a Princess Di. Women like this exist in high places. All the time. She bought into a comfort zone, and not just materially. She says that she thought Louis could fix everything, he's a doctor, he'll heal everything. And she finds out he's just a man.

Q: There was a clue to Louis' character in the script, where you have him trace a line down someone's cheek. Sam Jackson made that a promiscuous gesture of Louis's; he touches all women's cheeks that way.

A: Sam got that. It's in the script, and it was a key to the character, but Sam Jackson really got it. Sam got Louis.

Q: When creating a character, will you try to find a visual or symbolic gesture that will illuminate that character? Like Mozelle, the seer who has a blind spot to her own life.

A: It's poignant to me when there's something about a person that's their idiosyncrasy, or their weakness. To me, for Louis, it's that he's supposed to be a healer but he's destroying the things that he loves. He loves his family, but he can't help himself.

Q: The scenes in the script where Roz and Louis touch were cut, so they end up a married couple that barely touch.

A: They actually have a very beautiful scene that was shot, and it's one of the few things that I changed because of test screenings. Most of the time test screenings proved to me things I always knew were true, like: yeah, the audience is supposed to be uncomfortable here. I was always defending the audience's reaction to the movie. That was one specific place where I got a reaction to a scene that I didn't want. It was such a beautiful scene, but maybe it pushed the limits of melodrama. People just didn't want to see Roz go there, because they're mad at

Louis. It happened consistently, every time it was screened. I would have loved to have kept it in, but I felt that it was hurting Roz's character, in a way. First I had it in another place in the movie, and they made me move it. So then it was in the movie but not where it is in the script. In moving it, the love scene happened too quickly after they had fought, right after the other woman calls the house. So the audience doesn't want to see her go there.

Q: Even though in real life sometimes it works that way.
A: Exactly, but the audience wants her to hang on to her anger a little bit. It felt like too weak a moment, too melodramatic.

Q: Who was Tomy supposed to be, and why was he cut? I felt like he was the watcher; the silent witness.
A: He was the mute witness. He means a lot to me. He's somebody from my childhood. The two characters in the story that remind me of someone in my family are mythicized characters, mythical versions of real people, and that's Mozelle and Tomy. I grew up with someone like Tomy. I'd have to go upstairs and say good night to him. It said a lot about Southern families, and African American families. You could have an invalid living in your house. You didn't put people in homes. Also, I liked having that piece of illness, of degeneration, in a family with that kind of beautiful exterior. They forced me to cut it.

Q: What was the explanation?
A: I don't know. Mark Amin (*head of Trimark*) gave me a lot of explanations, but I think it just rubbed him the wrong way. And it's true—one thing we were always in danger of was pushing the edge of melodrama, of gothic melodrama.

Q: All memories have witnesses, in a sense, and what's beautiful in that scene of Mozelle and the mirrors is that she's left standing alone, a witness to that memory. Tomy resonated on many levels, but also in that thematic sense.
A: And filmically, he really did. We used that. We shot him, it was very filmic. It makes sense, we loved it. The guys that did my sound used to joke about making an *Eve's Bayou* T-shirt with an empty wheelchair on the back, and it would say, "Where's Tomy?" It was one of the last big cuts that we made.

Q: *Eve's Bayou* has aspects of a gothic mystery. You open with a "body," when Eve says, "I killed my father," and you scatter clues as to why, at the party—with rivalries, jealousies, and betrayals. I thought Tomy was important in that he became the only guy that knew the truth.

A: He was. We loved it, but some people really didn't like it. I think Mark said that the character didn't pay off. We thought we had paid him off in the last scene. Mark thought, you see him and he disappears. It's true, people would watch the film at the test screenings and say, what's with the old guy? But someone else would say, well, he was the mute witness. So they would question it, but answer their own questions. It would promote a conversation, but maybe that was seen as not being a good thing. Test screenings are a very weird process to go through.

Q: Do you think that they damage films?
A: Oh, yeah.

Q: And everyone knows that, but they keep doing it anyway?
A: No, I think people don't know that. I think people absolutely believe in the numbers. Mark, for instance, would say, but Kasi, numbers don't lie. And I would say, Mark, numbers lie all the time! *Eve's Bayou* never tested well. But I'm sure now that people will mention *Eve's Bayou* in terms of test screenings and numbers not telling the whole story. Addis-Wechsler, who executive-produced *Eve's Bayou*, they said: none of our movies have ever tested well. *The Player* didn't test well, *Sex, Lies, and Videotape* didn't test well. Their attitude was that numbers *always* lie. But many people in Hollywood really believe in numbers.

Q: In speaking of your early work, including the script for *Eve's Bayou*, you once said that it was work done before you "knew the rules," and so you were therefore freer, and more open to certain rhythms. Is that something you'd recommend to young screenwriters?
A: It definitely helped me. Because it gives you strength, so that even after you know the rules, you have that strength. It's not that now I won't take any chances—now I want to take more chances. Because I'm bolstered. I'm encouraged by what I did then, when I wasn't afraid. The thing about *Eve's Bayou* is that I wrote it completely for myself, and that's advice I'd give anybody. Write from your heart, completely for yourself, as if nobody else is ever going to see it. And then maybe you can tweak it and adjust it later. If you write trying to second-guess what other people will like, you're shot.

Q: The opening lines, "Memory is a selection of images, some elusive ..." put me in a frame of mind where I was questioning the truth of each scene. In the party scene, I thought, is this a glamorized version of a party from Eve's memory? Did you intend that questioning POV in the viewer, that of seeing reality but also perhaps seeing through someone's memory?

A: Particularly Eve's point of view. I was trying to exactly re-create a look, from my memory. The story is made-up, but in defending the glamor of *Eve's Bayou*, I was trying to re-create what my parents and their friends looked like to me as a child. They looked like gods. And they were, in fact. If I look at pictures of them, they were gorgeous. And I wondered—why don't I see this in movies? When I was a kid, my parents were fabulous! Their hair was fabulous, they were really dressed, their friends were gorgeous, their parties were fabulous. I could show you pictures, you'd be knocked out, they looked like movie stars. I thought, why don't I see this in films? Why do I always see sweaty, "tore down" women? Is that supposed to be some authentic look? Of course, it is an authentic look, but it's not the full story.

Q: There is a sense of *Eve's Bayou* existing in a bubble all its own, immune from racism and sociological problems. Did you mean it to be a kind of mythic town?
A: Oh yeah, I did. But I wanted to tell a very complicated story. These are choices I made. I can write a million stories about racism in America. I've experienced it, I've been a Black woman every day of my life. It's a hard reality. It's not that I'm shutting my eyes to that. But this is a choice I made to tell a human drama with a one hundred percent African American cast, and if I was successful, anyone would be able to watch it and say, oh, that reminds me of my family. Because I think there is a human core there that is universal. On the other hand, like I said, I was writing for my soul. The flip side of saying the story is universal is to say that there was a period of my life, when I was a child, when I did not think of white people. If you had been to one of my parents' parties, I would have assumed that you were "colored," like everyone else. We lived in a Black world. Many people did, in the South, especially then. It's not that racism didn't occur, it's just that it wasn't an everyday subject of conversation. White people love to think that Black people are obsessed with them, and in many cases it's just not true. In many cases, people live in isolated worlds where they have their own fashion, they have their own upper class, they have their own lower class.

Q: Your film was praised for being an African American film that didn't paint the usual portrait of violence, that it told a normal human drama.
A: I think it's tricky. It's not that I wanted to ignore something. I always wanted to tell a complicated story with these characters. *Eve's Bayou* was always *Eve's Bayou*. There was a short story that I had written, that was about the original Eve, and Jean Paul Batiste giving her this land, and about how everyone could claim to be their descendants.

Q: Yes, when the script says she had sixteen children, I wondered, does that mean she begat the entire town?

A: Yes, she begat the town! People come in and marry into them, and become a mix of them, an amalgamated people.

Q: There's a wonderful, circuitous sense of justice in the story—it's a bullet that fells Louis, yet other things, too. You said earlier that your friends would exclaim, oh, he was killed with voodoo! I ended up thinking it was the emotional power of Eve herself, that it was more like personal voodoo.

A: That's exactly it. That was exactly my intention. I mean, I hate to be pinned down, I get wiggly about pinning down my intention in *Eve's Bayou*, because I do believe all things, all aspects of interpretation. But that's as close as anybody's ever come, really, to saying what my intention was. And the way I've always explained it was, two things: One, if you say, "Drop dead, Daddy," and your father drops dead the next day, how much do you feel responsible, your whole life? But also, putting a very strong thought out there, having a very strong thought, is that personal voodoo? Does it set things into motion? Is it to be avoided?

Q: You reinforce that idea on many levels. To me, the film is about the power of familial fidelity. The romance, and damage done, is between family members.

A: It's about lines crossed, it's about boundaries, and lack of boundaries. That's part of creating an insular world. The Batistes are so isolated, they're so bizarre that a boy gets killed, in their very small town, and they think, "We're free!" To me, that scene defines how weird they are. What a strange family, they live only within their own family. I have one friend with a completely opposite background, a white woman who grew up in Seattle, who talks about her family that way, in that they had their own rules. They were a tribe, they didn't need anybody else. The girl that plays Eve, Jurnee Smollett, her family is a little bit like that. They've got their own way of doing things. And that's what the Batistes are about. They're isolated, they're their own world.

Q: Cisely doesn't seem aware that her acceptance of her father's infidelities is something that she's learned from her mother. She's becoming her mother?

A: It's very intentional. She cuts her hair, she looks like her mother. But basically, I'm trying to say that that's dangerous. There are lines that shouldn't be crossed, and you have to be careful with children. Even if you love each other, you can love each other too much. They're so tight, they're enmeshed.

Q: I never felt like the script was moralizing or judgmental, and yet I did feel there was a touch of a cautionary tale.

A: Yes, but I don't like when it's called a cautionary tale. I resist that, I'm not trying to tell a cautionary tale, I'm telling a tale of a family who loved each other so much that they crossed boundaries. Things happened that they never meant to have happened.

Q: What was the inspiration to go for that very taboo, Elektracomplex moment of a father/daughter kiss?
A: It was always the story that I was telling. That moment has many sources. I was at a party once, of family friends, close friends, with a friend, when I was young. We were two twelve-year-old girls, doing champagne in the kitchen, and we came into the party, and said, "Let's flirt with the men!" And my friend sat on this man's lap, and a few minutes later, they were kissing. It was this weird moment where everything went in slow motion, and no one believed what they were seeing! Time stood still. And then everybody freaked out, and started screaming, people got kicked out, parents were mad, she got thrown in a cold shower. And when both people involved were questioned, they said they just found themselves in this moment, and that they didn't really know how it happened. Of course, toward this man, we were just incensed. We said, "You can never come into this house again!" It was this interesting, time-stood-still moment, where nobody believed their eyes. I was interested in that moment, and thinking that a moment can get away from you, and you're so horrified that you retreat behind fabrication.

Q: Cisely's POV shows, from a young girl's eyes, that romantic moment just before her father topples off the pedestal she's put him on. It's beautifully orchestrated from within her fantasy, so that you're never really sure what happened. Did both their versions happen?
A: Right. Something neither of them meant to happen, happened. And they were, like all good people, ashamed and horrified. They're not bad people, none of them are bad people, because bad people are not interesting. Sometimes they are—so, okay, let's make a movie about a serial killer. But most people are not bad, most people are just complicated. Life is complicated, and so to me it's more interesting that these aren't bad people.

Q: Could you talk about the evolution of the scene with Mozelle and the mirrors? In the first version of the script, Mozelle just tells the story in a monologue, in the second script that I read, you added the mirrors and the images out of the past.
A: It was very scary, because I had Mozelle talking for so long. There were going to be people who looked at this script, and this is their job, they know how to make movies, but they're going to say, "You've got a B-character talking for five minutes, what are you doing? These are pretty words, but do we really need it

in the movie?" We had to decide—what did we absolutely need in the movie to make it *Eve's Bayou*? It was my job to convince them that we needed that scene. But it was hard to articulate why, because you can excise it and still have the plot. So we tried to find a way to make it visually exciting. Also, in some ways, it's the defining scene of *Eve's Bayou*. It's not what it's about plot-wise, but it's the place where we see the past and its images.

Q: Where the two realities bridge. Speaking of bridges, I thought they were a wonderful symbol for crossing into other worlds.

A: That's another thing that's hard to describe, and maybe I'm not great at articulating why I want things, and I wish I was better at it because there were times when I was fighting for those bridges, fighting for a character to just walk through space. For me, every time a character walked, it meant something. And yet, that's not the way we're used to editing films these days. It's just seen as empty space, she's just walking. But you cross a bridge and you go to another place. In my little map of *Eve's Bayou*, the bridges also have meaning, logistically.

Q: The bayou, for you, is a symbol of fate, and history, I imagine? I noticed more water was added in, from script to film.

A: Yes, we put more water in. The bayou was always a character in *Eve's Bayou*. But we filled as much of the movie with water as we could. When Roz says, "I left my family and I moved to this swamp," I wanted you to just feel the swamp.

Q: So it worked also to help create the insular world you wanted?

A: It works for me on many levels. It's pools of memory, the trees are secretive and claustrophobic. In the script it says, of the bayou, "It's dark, secretive, and painfully beautiful." And that was really important to me. The water is dark, and reflective. You can't see through it, but it reflects. If you look into it you see dark shapes. The bayou is very, very beautiful, and old, and melancholy.

Q: You used black-and-white for the opening sequence. Was that to take you from the elder Eve's story to the young Eve's?

A: Yes, that was to take you from the past history to the present. My editor, Teri Shropshire, came up with the tree wipe, where you wipe the tree and you go from black-and-white to color. We decided that we'd go from mono to stereo, so the world opens up. The black-and-white is in mono, and then it passes the tree, and you go into color and into stereo, on Eve's line, "I was named for her." It has a spooky feeling as the world opens up.

Q: To get back to the idea of walking, your short film *Dr. Hugo* opens and closes on his feet, his walking, just like a Western—the stranger enters the town.

A: I have a thing about walking. In what I'm working on now I have people walking, and the way people walk means something to me. *Dr. Hugo* was interesting, because when I decided that I wanted to direct *Eve's Bayou*, Cotty (Caldecot Chubb), the producer, and I had been working on it for a while, trying to get it made. Cotty said, "Let's make a short film, a drama, that is going to remind people of *Eve's Bayou*, to show people what you might do. Give them a taste." We had taken this little scene of Louis doctoring out of *Eve's Bayou*, and Cotty said, could you expand that little scene? It was just a scene of Louis doctoring, of the beautiful woman in the bed, she coughs, and the door shuts, and that was it. So we wanted to make that into its own full piece that had its own integrity. It was an incredible act of good sense and valor on the part of Cotty Chubb. He produced half of the film out of his own pocket and my agents lent me the rest.

Q: So do you think that without that kind of support, would *Eve's Bayou* still be sitting around in the script stage?

A: Without Cotty Chubb and Sam Jackson, *Eve's Bayou* would still be sitting around in a script stage. It shows what can happen when there's passion behind a project. The first person that read the script was my then-boyfriend, now-husband, Vondie Curtis-Hall. He convinced me to show it to an agent. The only agent I knew was my acting agent. He asked the literary department to read it as a favor. Frank Wuliger is the agent that read it. Cotty and I shopped the script around for years. Everyone liked it, loved it, but no one was breaking down my door to make it. At first we were looking for other directors, but fortunately no one jumped. So I woke up, on my birthday, and decided I wanted to direct it. Cotty produced the short for me, to see if I had the "chops." Amy Vincent shot the short with me. Samuel Jackson saw the short and read the script and wanted to play the role. So now we had a package of sorts—me, Amy, Cotty, and Sam. A producer named Margaret Matheson got the script to Trimark. A brilliant man named Ray Price had recently joined the Trimark team to help them develop an art film division. Bobby Rock and Ray Price are responsible for bringing the script in. Mark Amin gets the credit for green-lighting the movie, with a first-time, Black woman director, who was nine months pregnant. It took a lot of faith. The budget was about four million, which is more than anyone else would have given us, even if they had been inclined to make the movie, which they weren't. I'll always be grateful.

Q: And in Dr. Hugo, you captured an essence that's in the longer film—the sense of the triangle of illicit behavior, between two adults and seen through a child's eyes.

A: It was something worth investigating. I want to go back to something you said about the point of view being slightly fantastical. It's interesting because, after I'd written the script, I saw two movies. I saw *The Piano* and *Like Water for Chocolate*. Both reminded me of what I was trying to accomplish. In *Like Water for Chocolate*, the whole story is a fantastical memory, it's like interpreting your past and making it folklore. And in *The Piano*, in that a child tries to make the world fair. Eve tries to make things fair and right with the world. Which of course you can't.

Q: Was Cisely's mistake putting the meting of justice into the hands of someone who was a little too powerful?
A: Exactly.

Q: Casting Diahann Carroll, the first Black woman to have a TV series, was wonderful. Was Elzora a good-willed character?
A: I have a question there, too. I can see it from both sides. I think she dislikes the Batistes. They're all from the same tribe, and yet she's poor. Mozelle is this beautiful woman with all this mystery around her, she has money and men. I think Elzora genuinely dislikes them, particularly Mozelle. However, I think Elzora's the kind of person, if a little girl comes to her and says, "I want to kill someone in my family," Elzora wonders, are you certain? Elzora takes Eve's money—that's the kind of woman she is. But even in 1962, twenty dollars is not enough money to kill somebody. Her sense of justice is that, for that thought, that you want to kill somebody in your family, you should be taken. I'm going to scare the hell out of you. Also, Elzora has a genuine power. When she says to Roz, "Look to your children," she's really talking from her soul. She says, "Sometimes a soldier fall on his own sword." What she's saying is not so much this is the day he's gonna die, but something bad's gonna happen to that man. He's slept with too many women in this town.

Q: There were several places in the script where characters got slapped that were cut. Why was that?
A: Oh, there was a lot of slapping and crying. (laughs) I love melodrama, but you don't want the audience to run screaming from the theater. You want them to sit through the movie. You want to use just enough, and that is also the fun of it. The fun of it is watching a child act, and knowing exactly how much emotion is the right amount. People always say, how did you get the children to cry? Well, getting them not to cry, that's the tricky thing. They would have sobbed a lot, through many scenes, if I had let them. The trick is to pull it back, to be conservative with the emotions, so that you don't push the audience out of their seats.

Q: And the scene with the little boy and the cricket? What I loved was that since the kids are doing such adult things, it was good to be jolted with a sweet reminder that they're just kids.

A: We never shot that. There were these crickets, in Louisiana. In specific months the insects grow supersonic. They're tremendous. People tie strings around their necks and walk them. They all die by September. We had seen one of these crickets, and I put it into the script. We took it out, we didn't have time to shoot it.

Q: And the Shakespeare?

A: That's from my childhood. That's me and my sister, we read everything by Shakespeare, and we acted out all the parts, and she always got to be the girls and I always had to be the men. She was always Juliet.

Q: The end, from script to film, is the most different. In the script, there was a bit more healing, in terms of a wedding, and Roz remarrying. I thought it was very brave to not have the wedding and the happy lift it gave to a dark story.

A: We shot the wedding. It was a great idea to age the girls, and have time pass. We used the sisters of the actresses, which was a brilliant idea. They were great, but after looking at Megan (Megan Good, who plays Cisely) and Jurnee for the whole movie, you just do not want to see another actress. They're just so beautiful and so engaging. When we went to six years later, you just stopped caring. Something shut off. So we shot it again, we shot a different ending. I wrote the scene when Mozelle comes to the tree and says, "Last night I had a dream . . ." Which was a dream of mine. I wrote it the night before we shot it.

Q: I thought you were adjusting the dials on how happy the ending should be, bringing it down a notch, to a darker ending.

A: In the original script, Mozelle dies. Mozelle died in the first few drafts. She marries Grayraven, and we hear this all in a monologue, during the transition. Grayraven dies in an accident, and she hangs herself from the rafters of her attic. Tragedy!

Q: What films influenced you? I thought of *Rashomon*, in terms of how you can't know the truth of an event.

A: *Rashomon* was mentioned a lot to me after I wrote the script, but I still haven't seen it.

Q: What about *To Sleep With Anger*, or *Daughters of the Dust*?

A: I saw them after I wrote my script. *Daughters of the Dust* was one of those films where I said, oh, we speak the same language.

Q: I guess those are the obvious ones, but I'm curious if Ingmar Bergman was an influence. There's often a distant father . . .

A: Now that's another story. I'm a huge fan. The emotions are very painful, very heightened. It's hard to watch, it gets under your skin.

Q: How about literary influences? I think of Southern writers, Tennessee Williams and *To Kill a Mockingbird*.

A: I'm a huge Tennessee Williams fan. When I would describe Mozelle to the actress who played her, Debbi Morgan, I'd say, Mozelle's my Blanche Dubois. She's crazy, she's on this edge. Voices talk to her. And to Jurnee I would say, have you seen *To Kill a Mockingbird*? I made her watch it. Eve is my Scout. I wasn't copying their work, it's nothing like their work, but those characters definitely reminded me of something.

Q: You use a lot of symbols in your films. In the script, when Eve is making a voodoo doll of her father, she uses a snake, and she stabs it in the belly. That became a doll in the script?

A: It would have been nice if it were a snake in the film, but I can't remember why we lost that.

Q: And the spider web, is that fate, and Mozelle?

A: The spiders are very important, and Mozelle is the black widow. I'm working with this novelist, George Dawes Green, on a project, and moths are huge to him. Spiders are fascinating to me. I have a love/hate relationship with them. They freak me out, they haunt my nightmares. My mother's a psychologist, and she's always interpreting spiders variously as my enemies and other things. I remember once, staying at a house with Vondie, my husband, and there was a web in the corner, and a spider and her mate. We talked about them every day, because they were big and pretty. And then one day she ate him! We couldn't believe it, we were like, the bitch! She killed him! So that whole idea's in the film. It's not just black widows, but many spiders kill their mates. And their children eat them. Very interesting to me. *Eve's Bayou* is one of the fun places I could throw every single symbol that I'd ever thought about. It's funny, because lots of times people don't pick up on them. I did shamelessly blatant ones that fortunately not everybody gets. But every once in a while someone will say, Eve and the snake, Eve and the apple . . . *Eve's Bayou* was a fun place for symbols. Pomegranates symbolize death, and Mozelle says, "Let's eat them till our hands turn red!" But that's the kind of thing you might get self-conscious about later.

Q: That stuff just goes straight to the unconscious. That's where symbols come from, and in film they echo right back there.
A: I write from a semi-dream state, a lot. It's really my creative space. It's always been the way that I write. I go to bed thinking about a certain problem in a script, and I meditate, but in a sleep state. It's very freeing, and you get a lot of symbolism.

Q: Wasn't one version of the opening from a recurring dream?
A: That's from a very early draft, that was a dream from my childhood. A little girl is lying in the grass, and a bike wheel is spinning and everything is beautiful. She picks up a pretty little cricket, and when she opens her hands, spiders are crawling out from between her fingers. A silhouetted man appears in the distance and tells her she needs to come in. She can't see him, he looks big and dark against the sun. Then all the colors become very vivid, and she hears a voice, like a witch, saying something scary. It makes no sense, it's a dream. I thought it would be fun to put in a movie. It didn't make it very far at all.

Q: But the instinct, to imprint the audience with an opening that's primal and mysterious, a tableau out of the unconscious, that makes sense.
A: I still do that, in a way, with the black-and-white opening, it's still fragments of a memory, and what are you really seeing?

Q: Yes, but more literally tied into the story, rather than surreal.
A: Yes, it's more literal. I love the surreal, it's a huge part of my artistic life. Magic realism, surrealism and how they tie in to everyday life. There's so many people that are walking around tripping in their minds. It's a great thing to convey. I walk around tripping all the time. Not everybody is interested in this, some people are interested in realism, or vérité. And reality is good, too. But this is what I'm interested in. It's the kind of novels I'm interested in. The things that I most enjoy go to great heights.

Q: To get back to one more script-to-film difference, I wondered why the scene with Eve watching Matty and her dad moved out of the wine cellar and out into the carriage house.
A: The house we used didn't really have an interesting cellar. I wanted a dark, spooky, spidery cellar. But there was an outbuilding, a carriage house. One of our visual influences was a photographer named Clarence John Laughin. Amy Vincent introduced his work to me. He did a lot of spooky double-exposures. In some of his images, you can't tell what you're seeing, but in this one of a carriage, you feel that there's a dead woman in the carriage. We were definitely inspired by him.

Q: Why did you decide that this was a Southern tale? For the slow, sexy rhythms of the South?

A: Because the people are so colorful. And I came from a very Southern family. My mother was born in Americus, Georgia. My father grew up in Birmingham but was born in Louisiana. We shot the film in Madisonville and Covington, across Lake Pontchartrain from New Orleans. It is the rhythms, and the poetry, and a certain way of speaking, which many members of my family put behind them. (laughs) But also, even though it's not true, the South seems heightened, more dramatic, more emotional. A friend of mine said something brilliant about the South. He said, "The South is like Europe, the past oppresses the present." And, without going into the specific history of slavery, I wanted that sense of oppressiveness, and a rich past.

Q: Could we talk about your background? You're also an actor, and you've said, "Acting and writing together, the natural marriage of that is directing."

A: In a sense, yes. Writing is acting for me. I act all the roles I write. I act them, to myself, in my mind. And directing is writing. When you write you're directing it. I'm trying to put into writing what I see. So it's not necessarily that the directing comes out of the marriage of acting and writing, it's that they're all intertwined. It makes sense, that if you're an actor that writes, you should direct. Acting is totally visceral. It's being an emotional creature, a creature of instinct and technique together. It's being an emotional entity that morphs with the moment. Writing is control. Writing is saying what you see. And directing is capturing the whole thing, the emotion and the words, and presenting it.

Q: And other scripts, what about *He Ain't Dead Yet*?

A: I wrote that in 1980 with my girlfriend Billie Neal, a novelist and an actress. *Eve's Bayou* was the first thing I wrote by myself; then I became a studio writer, which is still my bread and butter.

Q: What does that term mean exactly, "studio writer"?

A: Screenwriter for hire. I write for a living now, I write for studios. *Eve's Bayou* is negative money, you lose money doing those.

Q: For studio assignments, they give you an idea, a scenario?

A: Yeah, they'll give you a sentence. Or two words, or three words. For *Still Life*, it was "modern *Bride of Frankenstein*." And then I write something completely far out. Universal owns the title, *Bride of Frankenstein*, and so they thought, I wonder if someone could do something interesting with that? They wanted an interesting new *Bride of Frankenstein*. (laughs) And then the fun is to write the last thing they could possibly expect.

Q: You wrote scripts for Whitney Houston and Michelle Pfeiffer?
A: *Privacy*, for Michelle Pfeiffer, and *For Josette*, for Whitney Houston. None of these scripts have been produced yet.

Q: Are you being turned to now, to write great parts for women?
A: Sure, I guess. I've written so many different kinds of things, at this point. I was very fortunate that before people knew who I was, I'd written *Privacy*. Michelle Pfeiffer and her producing partner, Kate Guinzburg, were incredibly brave and innovative, because based on the strength of the women characters in *Eve's Bayou*, they hired me to write a completely urban, edgier story.

Q: For an all-white cast? Was that an interesting writing switch?
A: It's not that different. I mean, as a Black person living in a modern world, you know all about it, you understand the "master race." For white people to under-stand enough to write like a Black person, that might be different, because white people don't have to understand Black people. Black people have to understand white people. You know what I mean? (laughs) So it's no big deal for me. People are basically people, there might be a certain different rhythm, but I'm going to hear that rhythm a billion times a day, so I'm going to be able to write it.

Q: Are you working on a new script, something personal?
A: They're all personal, but not like *Eve's Bayou*. I don't know if anything's go-ing to be like *Eve's Bayou*, that was the one. They're all deeply personal. If they weren't, it wouldn't be fun.

Q: You've said, "*Eve's Bayou* is personal, not autobiographical."
A: Yes. I feel that writing, if it's good, should be embarrassing. It should ache. Because it's so personal, it should ache.

(Kasi Lemmons was interviewed by Annie Nocenti at Motor City Films, on the 20th Century Fox lot.)

Caveman's Valentine:
I Just Like to Stir It Up a Little

Cynthia Fuchs / 2001

From *Nitrateonline.com*, March 9, 2001. Reprinted by permission.

Kasi Lemmons laughs warmly and often. Witty, passionate, and gracious, she's also comfortable with contradictions, chatting easily in New York's Regency Hotel, wearing her signature blond dreadlocks and a business suit; after the interview, she puts her arm around you to say good-bye and thank you, like she means it.

Born in 1961 in St. Louis, Missouri, Lemmons decided early that she wanted to act, and took up dancing as a means to improve her acting. She began her movie career early: at eighteen she played a "Hostage" in *11th Victim*, a TV movie directed by Jonathan Kaplan. From there, she appeared in a series of memorable movies (*School Daze, Silence of the Lambs, Fear of a Black Hat*) and TV series (*Cosby, Walker, Texas Ranger* [!]). All the while, she was also writing scripts—she calls writing her "straight job." Currently, Lemmons and her husband, actor-director Vondie Curtis-Hall (*Gridlock'd*), split their time between making films and raising their four-year-old son and sixteen-month-old daughter, but it wasn't so long ago that Lemmons was a new talent. In 1997, she wrote and directed the lovely and innovative *Eve's Bayou*.

In Lemmons' highly anticipated second film, *The Caveman's Valentine*, written by George Dawes Green and based on his Edgar Award-winning novel, Samuel Jackson plays Romulus Ledbetter, a homeless man and former piano prodigy who solves a murder mystery.

Cynthia Fuchs: *The Caveman's Valentine* is populated with characters who don't get much play in mainstream movies—the homeless, a crazy man, sexualized middle-aged characters, interracial sex, a Black woman with a gun, gay men, and an upscale art scene, all in a film that's considerably bigger than your first one. Was it difficult to put all these elements together?

31

Kasi Lemmons: Well, it's a bigger film than *Eve's Bayou*, but still in a medium-to-small budget range. It is a very ambitious movie, though, very dense. And even though you're dealing with some difficult things—homelessness, junkies, homosexuality, and marginally, the S&M avant-garde art scene—there's this Alice-Through-the-Looking-Glass quality, like you just fell into a world, that made me think it was very beautiful. I thought that the fact that the Caveman was a voice for a disenfranchised population, a fringe-dweller, was really moving.

CF: The multiple layers come in part from the novel on which it's based, which takes place mostly inside Rom's head. How do you translate that kind of subjectivity to film?

KL: That's sort of the fun of it. It's something that appeals to me. And it's a big question to answer, for me. When I was in film school in New York in 1987, I made a short film called *Fall from Grace*, seven minutes long, about homeless people. And I didn't know any better, I didn't know the rules, how you make documentaries or anything like that. So I would make sandwiches for some people and ask, "Do you mind if I sit here this afternoon and film you?" Some of them minded and some didn't and the ones that didn't, I would take my camera with a long lens across the street and kind of spy on them, wait until they forgot I was there. Part of the reason I wanted to make the film then was that the White House had recently decided to release a lot of people from mental institutions, and they ended up on the streets of New York, suddenly. What I captured in this short film was this extraordinarily dynamic life that was going on with these people, that you could photograph, but you couldn't get inside. It was so compelling, and in a sense it was so much not what I expected, because what I wanted (and I got that too) was this one-step-over-the-line, slipping into darkness, you just made a single mistake and things get out of control for a second, and you're homeless. But there was something else—I got a lot of people talking to themselves, talking to the sky, screaming at the sky. And as you're watching you know, obviously, something is going on that is big for this person, and I wanted to know what that thing was. So, cut forward to years later, and I get this script for *The Caveman's Valentine* and I have the opportunity to imagine and express what somebody like this is seeing and thinking and feeling. George (Dawes Green) had written this from his book, and the character is so beautifully drawn in the book, he's a mythic character, a millennium mythic character, something you haven't seen before. I fell in love with Romulus Ledbetter.

CF: How did you come to the final script, between you and George?

KL: He wrote the first two drafts, I wrote the next three, and he wrote the last one and I rewrote it, so we worked on it together, but it's George's script. Even when I was working on it, it was as a director, shaping the visual language.

CF: As you write, even your own original scripts, do you think in terms of images?
KL: Yes, absolutely. I am a screenwriter for a living, it's my straight job. But unless you're writing for yourself, it's not great form to write that way, because you want to leave it blank for the director, but that's the way it presented itself to me. So people would say, "Can you pull that back?" Now that I write for myself, I put it all in, because it's like directing it.

CF: Clearly, the directing is working out for you—do you pursue directing projects?
KL: No, it's almost like the ones that I'm involved in, I found a long time ago or they found me, and it's something that I've just attached to. Somebody will say, "Have you read that book?" and I'll say, "Oh, I love that book!" I haven't reached out for anything new in a long time. One of the other things I'm involved with is a story I've been following for fifteen years, and another is a script I wrote a long time ago when I was writing for a living, that has now come back to me with an offer to direct it. If I could only do the projects that I'm interested in now, and then retire (laughs), that'd be okay too.

CF: Can you talk some about the women characters in *The Caveman's Valentine*? Though Romulus is so huge as a presence, the women, especially, to me, his daughter Lulu (played by Aunjanue Ellis), are so carefully delineated. How different are they from the novel?
KL: The relationship between Romulus and Lulu is a big difference actually. It's something that George and I went back and forth on, and now we agree. I felt very strongly about it—the relationship in the book is much sweeter. I thought it would be interesting and appropriate if she was really embarrassed. She's trying to make a living, and to toe the line—she's a Black woman cop in New York, you talk about being in a man's world, and the sh*t she has to hear, about her dad and everything else. I felt it was such a great opportunity for dramatic tension. In the book, it's very beautiful. I gave it an arc, which I felt was realistic and could be painful in a good way. I have a father-daughter thing, and it can be such a beautiful relationship. It's so primary, and is so great to write about.

CF: You never see Sheila (played in the film by Tamara Tunie) except from the back, on the edge of the frame, or as a projection from Romulus.
KL: She's his version of Sheila. That was a big question, and not in the book. But I thought about it a long time, and realized that I would be driving down

the streets of Los Angeles and seeing people I knew from high school, and then realizing it wasn't them, but people who looked like how I remembered them. When you picture somebody you haven't seen in seventeen years, you don't age them conspicuously, the way that they would have aged. You imagine them the way that they were, but less realistic version, because memory is subjective. So he remembers her as what we called "Sheila Fabulous," the best part of him, the sanest voice of his. She challenges him but she also encourages him.

CF: One her most striking visitations comes when he's having sex with Moira (Ann Magnuson).
KL: And that was a gas to direct! She sits on the bed, his ex-wife, and his reaction is just perfect, the way he played it. He was like "Go away!" (laughs)

CF: How were you thinking about that relationship between Moira and Romulus?
KL: I love Moira. She went through a lot of changes from the book, along the lines of, how not to kitschify her? And yet, she's this free spirit, living on the fringe of her brother's fame and that whole world, but she's this earthy, sexy person. She's kind of rock'n'roll, she's got a bit of an edge and she's sexy, she doesn't give a f*ck. She has a lot of humanity, marching to her own drummer, and I love that in a person, and in a woman.

CF: Did you give any thought to the recent controversies over interracial relationships on screens, say, over Eriq LaSalle's (as Peter Benton) brief liaison with Alex Kingston (as Elizabeth Corday) on *ER*?
KL: Well, you know, television is very interesting, there's a built-in conservatism, and you're bound to represent because there's so few characters (of color). But for me, it's wonderful. Anything provocative is good, to a certain extent. And all kinds of people sleep together—it's very human. My parents are interracial, my mother married my stepfather when I was nine, so it's life to me. I would never shy away from it. But it's amazingly provocative. I knew it was, but when we tested this movie, people went nuts, especially because Rom's homeless, so there's this whole "sullying" thing. But to me, that's really, really fun. I just like to stir it up a little.

CF: Did you have that in mind when you began directing, that you could stir things up?
KL: Yeah, not in the way that other people might mean it. To me, *Eve's Bayou* is very edgy and radical and had never been done, a bold frontier. But you could easily look at it and say, "Oh, it's a quirky little film." It was very important that it was one hundred percent African American, because these are the people of

Eve's life. People asked me to put in white characters, and I would say, "Well, there aren't any. It's my bayou." To me that had its own power and stirred things up, but not in the way that *The Caveman's Valentine* might. That was an opportunity in so many ways—I designed the photographs: S&M, me? It was a great playground. At the same time, I knew I was pushing a lot of buttons and I tried to be a little classy about it, I didn't want to drive people screaming from theaters. But at the same time it was a great opportunity to explore life.

CF: Were you expecting controversy?

KL: Sure. There haven't been as many as I expected. Early on I decided that the only way to do this was to have a lot of heart. I thought, "If you're going to go direct *The Caveman's Valentine*, you've gotta go for it." At this point, I haven't seen anything that surprised me. Sundance is a wonderful place to show a movie like this, because you get a mixed audience, film buffs and film people and also people from the area, which is very Mormon. So I was pleasantly surprised at that reaction. It did well.

CF: You like the festival business?

KL: Oh I love it. It's a little bit of a panic, you can't relax, you're scared. But I've had great experiences, you meet people you wouldn't normally. At Telluride, when we took *Eve's Bayou*, there I was, walking around with John Sayles. And I went to Sundance, and Joan Chen became my pal, and Darren Aronofsky. It's cool. You get to talk about film with people you admire.

CF: So do you imagine that in the future, you'll be sticking with these smallish, festivalish films?

KL: Yes. But you never know. Some people might say that *Caveman's Valentine* is already too slick, you know what I mean? It has a polishedness that I like in my filmmaking. I tend to keep doing movies that are challenging stories and have a certain degree of not-your-average-movieness, because that's my taste.

CF: Part of the challenge is how you represent what's real and what's not, or how these blend together, for individuals. This film gave you a chance to focus closely on that slippage. Can you talk about the ways you decided to represent that, across varying visual registers?

KL: Yes, that's a big part of the fun. I get a certain idea when I'm going through the script and doing my director's version, so I put it in then, which is in black and white and whatever else. And that organizes the material visually. And then my DP (Amelia Vincent, with whom Lemmons also worked on *Eve's Bayou*) and I go through and refine that. So, at one point in the script, Rom refers to the Z-ray as being a "pernicious shade of green," and we had to decide what was pernicious enough. The most fun and the most challenging and the most heartache that I got in all of that was in Rom's skull. You know it's dark in there, it's spooky and like a basilica, it says in the book, but you have to figure out what it feels like. That was fun and painful, on our budget, and my production designer (Robin Standefer) pulled it out of her hat. It was a saga, of the wings and the space. It was an opportunity, because you don't often see Black angels, but it was also new territory—I decided the seraphs were sort of Rom's ancestors and his furies. The black and white, we used that for his flashes of instinct and insight, and Amelia came up with this stock that's very high contrast and difficult to work with, ASA 6, because you have to use such bright lights to make it work. The actors were literally squinting under those lights. But it has a beautiful and shocking look. Amelia and I get far into it—like, "What does instinct feel like? What does it look like?"—and then, we come back from it. We're so far into the visual thing, analyze it, storyboard it, know it thoroughly, and then, we think, "The actors are coming!" And then we can work with the actors.

CF: And what happens in that next step?

KL: You never know. That's filmmaking. You've got to be a little light on your feet, or you'll die. A good example in this film is, we were introducing Sheila on the street—Tom's looking at the poster wall and she comes up behind him. We were going to have her walk out of a background at the wrong speed, so the background would go into slow motion, and she'd come towards him in twenty-four (fps, normal speed). We'd have to bluescreen it, it was complicated, but we knew what we were doing, we were all set up. Well, there's a blizzard. And we can't bring Sheila in a blizzard. She's Sheila Fabulous and she's a vision, she can't have her hair a mess and snow in her eyes. So we had to think fast. We walked her down a ladder in the library. It would have been great to have her on the street, but there you have to adjust. It's the whole adrenalin-jumping-off-a-cliff thing.

Kasi Lemmons

Wheeler Winston Dixon / 2006

Dixon, Wheeler Winston. 2007. *Film Talk: Directors at Work*. New Brunswick: Rutgers University Press.

Kasi Lemmons is one of the new generation of African American filmmakers who grew up in the business working as an actor in everything from McDonald's commercials to series television and soap operas, and then moved on smoothly to the big screen in such films as Jonathan Demme's *Silence of the Lambs* (1991) and Bernard Rose's *Candyman* (1992). However, even while she was absorbed in building her career as an actor, she also worked diligently as a writer on her own unproduced projects and longed for a chance to direct her own film. That moment finally came with *Eve's Bayou* in 1997, a touching portrait of African American family life that became a huge crossover hit with mainstream audiences. The success of the film, which Lemmons wrote and directed, effectively put her on the map as a talent to watch.

Most recently, Kasi has been shooting *Talk to Me* (2007), with Don Cheadle and Cedric the Entertainer, and seems determined to continue to work as both an actor and a director for the foreseeable future. Married to the actor/director Vondie Curtis-Hall (*Waist Deep* [2006]), Kasi manages to balance the demands of family life, an acting career, and her own personal projects as writer/director. It seems that we have only just begun to hear from this immensely gifted woman. This conversation took place on March 22, 2006, and offers a view into the life of an artist who is constantly searching for the next project that will captivate her interest, whether as a writer, actor, or, as she makes clear she most prefers, director.

Wheeler Winston Dixon: You were born as Karen Lemmons. Why did you change your name to Kasi?
Kasi Lemmons: I never really changed it. Nobody ever called me Karen— a couple of people, my father occasionally. My mother and my sister always called me Kasi or Katie.

WWD: And so that just basically stuck?
KL: Yes.

WWD: You were born in St. Louis, Missouri, on February 24, 1961, but you were raised in Boston, Massachusetts, after your parents divorced. Could you tell me a little bit about your early life, your mother and father, and what they did?
KL: My father was a biology teacher, and my mom a counselor, and then she became a psychologist. And she finally got her doctorate in education at Harvard, which is why we moved to Boston after they got divorced, because she wanted to go to Harvard.

WWD: Were your parents supportive of your early work?
KL: Well, my mom put me in drama school, but I think that the reason was to occupy my time. She didn't want me to get depressed about the divorce.

WWD: How old were you when they got divorced?
KL: I guess I was nine.

WWD: What effect did that have on you?
KL: Well, I'm not sure that they got along very well. As a matter of fact, I'm sure they didn't. There's always a question of whether it's more stressful to have kids in a marriage when the people involved clearly don't get along. So in some ways I was a little bit relieved. Also, I had an adventurous nature, and for me, going to Massachusetts was kind of an exciting thing. So I can't say it was all bad.

WWD: When did you first decide that you wanted to act?
KL: Well, it was really when my mom put me into acting school.

WWD: Was that the Boston Children's Theater?
KL: Even before the Boston Children's Theater. It was just a drama class, but I thought, "Wow, this is fun." So I kept at it. It was almost like a daycare center where they played dramatic games.

WWD: What is the Boston Children's Theater like?
KL: Well, it was wonderful when I was a kid; they had several companies. There would be one company that would perform downtown in Boston at the big theaters. Then there was a touring company, which would go out on the road and do children's summer theater. We worked out of the back of a truck; it was very informal, but really fun. We had some very good actors, mostly between eight and sixteen. The older kids would get the great parts, and we would kind

of shuffle around and do the smaller parts. But it also functioned for me almost like an agency, because I got my first professional acting job out of Boston Children's Theater.

WWD: How did that happen?
KL: They were looking for a kid, so they called up people that worked with children in the area. It was a courtroom drama called *You Got a Right.* I played Catherine Cooper, the first Black girl to integrate a white school. So it was a historic show.

WWD: What happened next?
KL: While I was still in high school, I was very academic, and I went to a super-difficult school called Commonwealth; and in the summer I went to the Circle in the Square Program, a theater program. I was about fifteen, and that was the next place that I was with kids who kind of wanted to be professional actors.

WWD: And what kinds of plays did you do?
KL: At that time I was probably doing a lot of Shakespeare.

WWD: Do you have a favorite Shakespeare play?
KL: Well, I had a lot of fun doing *Lady Macbeth*, and I had a lot of fun being Ariel in *The Tempest.* And of course I played Juliet in *Romeo and Juliet.* That was a given. Well, the Circle in the Square was in New York, of course, and that was part of New York University's School of Drama at the time. So you could go out and do your acting classes at different studios. I would go to Lee Strasberg's studio or Stella Adler's. So later, when I was at NYU, I opened with Circle in the Square. Then I transferred from NYU to the University of California, Los Angeles, and went back into academics.

WWD: And what did you plan to do?
KL: I just wanted to continue my education. I was already working professionally as an actor, doing commercials and stuff of that sort.

WWD: Do you recall what commercials you did?
KL: A lot of them. I made my living doing commercials for a long time. I guess one of the most famous ones I did was for Levi's 501 blue jeans. I did a *lot* of McDonald's commercials while I was going to UCLA. So, I thought, "Well, I'll just finish up in subjects that I'm kind of interested in." So I did European history and became a sociology minor. But, I didn't really hang out at UCLA too long either. I came back to New York and went to The New School for filmmaking classes.

WWD: Your first film was *Fall from Grace*.
KL: Yes, I made that while I was at The New School, in 1987 or 1988.

WWD: But before that, when you were at UCLA, you got your first acting job in a movie, right?
KL: Yes, that was *The 11th Victim* (1979), directed by Jonathan Kaplan. I played a rape victim, and the film was based on the Hillside Strangler murders. It was my first real gig, so I think I was completely awful. I was terrified.

WWD: But you'd done all those commercials.
KL: It's different. This was more like acting—I got to scream and everything. It was exciting. The other stuff was just, "look at this hamburger."

WWD: The next thing I have for you is a *Spenser: For Hire* episode in 1985, entitled "Resurrection."
KL: Yes, that was in New York. That's after I'd been working with the Steppenwolf Theatre Company at the Minetta Lane Theatre in New York. John Malkovich was our director. Before that, I was getting "cute little girl" parts, but suddenly I was getting edgier material. For a while, that's what I wanted to do, and this helped me. A little bit tougher, a little bit edgier than the stuff that I had been doing. Then I got *Spenser: For Hire*, which was a series television episode, no more, no less.

WWD: Which led to an ABC Afterschool Special with Tempestt Bledsoe and Della Reese, *The Gift of Amazing Grace* (1986), in which you had one of the major roles, as Subaya. What did you learn out of that?
KL: I learned a lot about continuity. That was the first time that a continuity person ever came up to me and said, "Hey, I just wanted you to know, for your future as an actor, that you need to pay more attention to this." That was a wake-up call. There's lot of things you have to pay attention to.

WWD: Then you went on to some serious studio time with *As the World Turns* from 1986 to 1989 as Nella Franklin. What did all this work teach you? Was working on a soap good for your discipline and your ability to memorize and run lines quickly?
KL: Well, actually, it was very on and off—I mean *very* on and off. I wasn't on the soap every day; I reoccurred. I didn't even have a contract. It was more or less, "we need you now, so come in." It's good for just teaching you to be natural and to be able to say anything naturally.

WWD: And also to get through it because you can't stop, right?

KL: Yes.

WWD: It's sort of like being on stage, because cutting the camera costs a fortune. They do it all live with multiple cameras, so you can't screw up.

KL: The big thing I learned with soaps is that when your camera is on, there's a red light on it. And it's not like talk shows: you can't look at the camera; you have to avoid it. Just look upstage, downstage, whatever; but don't look at the camera, even for a second. You have to pretend it isn't there. But it helped that I had been doing theater for a while.

WWD: You were in Spike Lee's *School Daze* (1988), which I thought was a very interesting film, in a small part. What was that like?

KL: Oh, it was wonderful. That was my first meeting with Spike. We got along great; he was fantastic. Oddly enough, I just saw Spike last night, at the premiere of his new film, *Inside Man* (2006).

WWD: What can you tell me about the experience? How long were you involved in the shoot?

KL: I was probably there a week. That was shot in Atlanta, on the Morehouse campus. The greatest thing about that film was working with Sam Jackson and Branford Marsalis. It was a big step up.

WWD: You continued to do a lot of television to pay the bills: a two-part episode of *The Cosby Show* entitled "The Birth" in 1988; an episode of *The Equalizer* entitled "Day of the Covenant," also in 1988; and an episode of *A Man Called Hawk* entitled "Life after Death" in 1989.

KL: I'm sorry, but I really can't remember anything about those shows. It was such a long time ago. But I remember it was work and put food on the table.

WWD: Then you appeared in this rather strange film, *Vampire's Kiss* (Robert Bierman, 1989), with a pretty amazing cast (Nicolas Cage, Maria Conchita Alonso, Jennifer Beals, and Elizabeth Ashley), in which literary agent Peter Loew (Cage) believes that he's becoming a vampire. You're billed fifth in this, as "Jackie." It's your first starring role. How did this happen?

KL: I love *Vampire's Kiss*. I auditioned for it, and I got it. It was a big coup for me. It was a really cool film, and I had a blast. It was so much fun. That was my first lead, and the cast and crew were really tight.

WWD: And then back to the soaps: "Jackie" in *Another World* from 1989 to 1990. What prompted the move back to daily television-lack of decent roles in other projects?

KL: Yes, yes. It was money.

WWD: But then you began appearing in some really solid theatrical films in rapid succession in the early 1990s, such as Larry Peerce's *The Court Martial of Jackie Robinson* (1990), a TNT television movie; Jonathan Demme's *Silence of the Lambs* (1991), which we all know about; and Robert Townsend's very sweet valentine to the history of rhythm and blues, *The Five Heartbeats* (1991), way down in the cast list but working with Diahann Carroll and the Nicholas Brothers. You also appeared in Larry Elikann's feature film *The Great Los Angeles Earthquake* (1991). Was this a conscious decision to move away from television? What can you tell me about these projects?

KL: Well, Larry Peerce was great. At first I thought he was an intimidating guy, but it was just a first impression. He's a lovely, lovely guy, and we see each other.

WWD: And *The Silence of the Lambs*?

KL: Well, that was a huge moment in my life. Everybody who was associated with that film suddenly had enormous visibility; it was just a monster. It was huge in a lot of ways, and Jonathan (Demme) also took me under his wing a little bit on the press junkets and stuff like that. He thought it would be good for my education to participate as much as possible. He invited me to the Oscars; I was there when it won for Best Picture (in 1992, along with Best Director for Demme, Best Actress for Jodie Foster, Best Actor for Anthony Hopkins, and Best Adapted Screenplay for Ted Tally). And so we became kind of quite close. I think it's easy when movies have, at least in one location, a contained cast. This was also true later of *Candyman* (Bernard Rose, 1992) and, before *The Silence of the Lambs*, on *Vampire's Kiss*. We were kind of a contained group, and so we got quite close. It's an extended family.

WWD: At this point you've been working with lots of different directors. Is there anyone in particular from whom you are picking stuff up? Are you thinking about being a director at this point?

KL: I was starting to think about being a director. But when I was acting, I was very focused on acting; I was trying to be technically perfect. I can remember on *The Silence of the Lambs* not being able to hit a mark correctly that I had to get in a scene with Jodie, which was right before lunch. Of course, she could have hit it in her sleep. We had to come down some stairs and we're looking at a television, and for some reason we never quite got it—or I never got it—and

I remember just kind of dwelling on that and how important it was to hit the marks *exactly*.

WWD: What about Robert Townsend's *The Five Heartbeats*?
KL: I love that. I loved working with Diahann Carroll and the Nicholas Brothers; it was a blast. By this time, I'm kind of cruising in my career; I've done a lot of work, and I'm very comfortable. These are my friends; I know a lot of them. So it was a lot of fun. That was a comfortable set.

WWD: *The Great Los Angeles Earthquake*?
KL: Oh, I had just come out to LA, and I took all the jobs. Why not?

WWD: Then suddenly you broke through in a very interesting horror film, Bernard Rose's *Candyman*, as "Bernadette Walsh." This was several cuts above the usual thriller; Tony Todd was fantastic in the lead role. How did you get involved in this?
KL: Bernard is very "imitable" as a director: most people who work with him can do an imitation of him. But he's lovely. We actually became quite close friends. I became friends with a lot of directors I worked with, and the producers.

WWD: Tony Todd was amazing in this movie as the Candyman, a sort of urban boogeyman, and the film was a major horror hit. Did you know that this was going to have such an impact when you were involved in it?
KL: No, I never did.

WWD: Is it like this with all your films? Do you ever know in advance how it's going to come out in the end?
KL: No, I never do.

WWD: Not even *The Silence of the Lambs*?
KL: No. It was just like, "Here we are, we're doing this movie, and that's that." So, yes, I was surprised when it broke through and became a cult favorite. You just never know when you're working on the set what it's going to be like when it's completed.

WWD: Then you were in the first US film directed by John Woo, *Hard Target* (1993), a Jean-Claude van Damme vehicle that was the victim of a lot of studio recutting, much to its detriment. But you were still working with good actors like Lance Henrickson, Wilford Brimley, and Arnold Vosloo. What was working on that project like?

KL: Well, I'm afraid I probably don't even know all the stories. John Woo and I became friendly, and I was good friends with Lance Henrickson. I was having a pretty good time. I usually had a really good time with people I was working with. I can't even remember that not being the case.

WWD: Some more television followed: an episode of *Murder, She Wrote* entitled "The Survivor" in 1993; and even a *Walker, Texas Ranger* episode, "Night of the Gladiator," also in 1993. Other than working with a nice ensemble cast in *Murder, She Wrote*, anything of interest here?
KL: It was series television, and I enjoyed it.

WWD: Then you did Rusty Cundieff's *Fear of a Black Hat* in 1994, which was a really interesting hip-hop comedy. How did you get hooked into that?
KL: Well, Penny Johnson (-Gerald), was supposed to do that; but at the last minute she got *The Larry Sanders Show*, so she couldn't do it. And so Rusty called me at the last minute and asked me if I would come in for that shoot. Now that was really funny. On that set, because I was working with comedians and kind of being the straight woman, I was thrown off balance a bit. So it was very challenging in a fun sort of way. I just laughed all the time.

WWD: Rusty Cundieff went on to score the next year with *Tales from the Hood* (1995), a very interesting social activism horror film; then he went on to do *Sprung* (1997), a romantic comedy. But then there's a big gap, and I'm shocked to see him reduced to directing *The New Adventures of Spin and Marty* for Disney in 2000. What happened?
KL: Well, I saw him last night, too, at the *Inside Man* premiere. Rusty has so much talent; he's really an enormously talented person, very prolific and relaxed about his style. He's done a lot of television, and I think he's really going to keep working in both features and television.

WWD: Which brings me to you. I keep hearing from your friends over and over again that basically you consider writing your real job, that you write all the time.
KL: It's true. I've been writing scripts all the time, pretty much every day for fourteen years. I write on the computer. I have to write scripts, because that's the only way I can write parts that will get a lot of people whom I really want to work with involved.

WWD: It seems to me that there's an enormous amount of talent in Hollywood, Black and white, that gets wasted. When you think of people like David Alan Grier, Clarence Williams III, Tisha Campbell, Robert Townsend, and many others, they're just not getting the roles they should. Why do you think this is? And why are there so few African American films being made?

KL: In (feature) films I think it's really difficult, because there is still this concept that Black movies don't sell overseas, which I don't believe. So it's still very, very difficult to get an African American film made. When there is one, what (the producers) want to know is, "Who can you put in it?" There is a very short list of people to choose from, so it makes breakout performances harder. They want A list stars to green light the film and to open it. Everybody is kind of looking for the star who is going to make their movie. So it makes it harder for new people.

The other problem is that the films aren't getting green lit in the first place. At the studio level, we don't quite have the executives we need. And then, when they are in there, they have to do what they think is going to help them keep their job and what makes sense for their company. Studios feel that African American movies don't sell overseas, for whatever reason, and they feel that the Black films will sell only to a certain segment of the population, and that's it. Once you go through that, there isn't going to be any crossover, especially with certain types of films. Which, of course, was one of the beautiful things about *Eve's Bayou* (1997)—we totally crossed over.

WWD: Yes, you absolutely did. Before you got into that, in 1994 you appeared in D. Clark Johnson's satire *D.R.O.P. Squad* (an acronym for "deprogramming and restoration of pride"), which had Spike Lee as executive producer and a great cast: Eriq La Salle, Vondie Curtis-Hall, Ving Rhames, and Vanessa A. Williams, among others. Is this where you first met Vondie Curtis-Hall, your husband, whom you married in 1995?

KL: Oh no, no, we'd known each other for a long time. I met him in a dance class in New York when I was a kid.

WWD: So when did the sparks start to fly?

KL: We were friends for a while, for maybe a couple of years. I think I met him when I was twenty, and we were just friends for a couple of years. But by the time I was making this film in 1994, we were already an item. Shooting *D.R.O.P. Squad* was a lot of fun; we shot it in Atlanta.

WWD: So when did you start working on the screenplay for *Eve's Bayou*, which was something you'd been interested in for a long time, correct?

KL: Probably about 1992.

WWD: What's your working method?

KL: Well, I had written a couple of screenplays by then, and I was a member of the Writer's Guild, but I had always been writing with somebody else. I had never really written one by myself. So it was kind of a big thing for me to embark on. It took a while to get it down. I would tell people the whole story at a party, way before I wrote anything down.

WWD: So you had the whole thing in your head?
KL: I had the whole thing in my head, and then it was just a matter of the discipline of actually sitting down and writing it.

WWD: How do you start your workday?
KL: I usually wake up and procrastinate for a while, and sometimes I get some exercise. Then I sit down, and I try and basically be in that space for about four to six hours. Every so often, I get up and take breaks. But I try and do a stretch of writing every day, and I actually am very possessive of my time. I look forward to a day where I don't have to do anything else, don't have a meeting, or work, or anything, to have just hours in front of me to work on a script. I get excited about it.

WWD: When did you decide that you were going to direct it? Did you just wake up one morning and say, "Hey, if I'm going to do this, I'm going to do it myself"?
KL: I woke up one morning literally, and it was an epiphany.

WWD: But first you had to direct the short film *Dr. Hugo* (1998), based on a segment of your script for *Eve's Bayou*, starring Vondie in the lead role, in order to convince the studios that you could direct *Eve's Bayou*. Why was this necessary after all the work you'd done before and behind the camera? Short film to convince them?
KL: Because I had just gone to film school and made these kind of semi-documentaries. I didn't have anything on film that resembled what was in my head.

WWD: Did you actually shoot film for *Dr. Hugo*, or did you shoot video?
KL: I shot film.

WWD: 35mm?
KL: Yes, 35mm. I mean, that was the whole point. It's kind of like, "OK, can you really do it, work with the cameras and a real crew and everything?" It took us about four days.

WWD: How did Samuel Jackson become involved?
KL: Well, Sam saw *Dr. Hugo*. Then he read the script, and at the time he was

playing a lot of character roles. He hadn't really done a leading man, somebody who gets the girl. He saw that this was a really good part for him, and so he got behind the project.

WWD: How would you describe the shoot for *Eve's Bayou*?
KL: Stressful and interesting. It was about thirty-six days.

WWD: Wow, that's pretty short.
KL: Yes.

WWD: And what was your budget?
KL: $3.8 million. Not that much.

WWD: Wow. And what was your shooting ratio?
KL: Oh, maybe three-to-one, two-to-one, something along those lines. (For every foot in the finished film, only two or three feet were left over of any given scene; average mainstream features usually have a ten-to-one ratio or even higher.)

WWD: Well, it looks absolutely gorgeous. We should give Amy Vincent, your director of cinematography, total props for her work on the film.
KL: Absolutely.

WWD: How did you hook up with Amy?
KL: Well, when I was looking for somebody to shoot *Dr. Hugo*, I was really looking for somebody who could emotionally tell a story through film. I knew exactly what I was looking for, and the producer, Cottie (Caldecot) Chubb and I went to the American Film Institute and looked at some shorts to see if we could find someone. We saw this short film, and it was so very moody, and a lot of it took place in a house. It was very moody, shadowy, and emotional, and we thought, "This might the person for us to shoot the movie." So she was the director of photography on *Dr. Hugo*, and then she was the DP on *Eve's Bayou*.

WWD: This was her first job as a DP on a feature, right?
KL: It was.

WWD: Wow. So this is a lot of faith.
KL: It was a lot of faith on the producer's part; and he really insisted, after we shot the short film together, on keeping us together. So it was a lot of bravery and faith on his part.

WWD: How did you keep the whole thing together when you were shooting it, just basically moving like crazy?

KL: Moving like crazy. I had the entire film visually in my head. Amy and I developed a real rapport on *Dr. Hugo*, so we could talk in shorthand. I mean, we could absolutely look at each other and communicate. She just got me. So we were able to kind of bring that to this film. Because we were trying for a look that we accomplished on *Dr. Hugo* we kind of knew what we were going for. And then we prepped it out: we storyboarded it, drew the whole movie.

WWD: So you storyboarded the whole thing?

KL: The whole thing.

WWD: That's a lot of work.

KL: So we were prepared. So, when things got crazy, we had a fallback plan, and we knew with each shot exactly what we were going for. But it was still very, very, very crazy. It was a tough shoot.

WWD: How long was Sam Jackson actually on the picture?

KL: Sam was on most of the run.

WWD: How did you feel when you wrapped shooting?

KL: Well, when we finished *Eve's Bayou*, I realized what it was going to be, and I thought it worked beautifully. But you never know if something is going to work for audiences. But it worked for me. And once I realized *that*, I felt that I never had to do it again, in a way. I felt, "Oh, I've done this. I've accomplished something." I did much more than I ever thought I could. I brought something from my head to an audience, and it was a wonderful feeling. And when it worked for the audience it was like having gone to heaven. It was just a magnificent thing. I guess as artists we really are searching for an audience, and you just want to communicate with them. So it was just really beautiful that the story found its way into other people's hearts. So in a sense I kind of felt, "OK, I don't have to direct again." And that lasted for about a minute. (Laughs)

WWD: Who released *Eve's Bayou*?

KL: Trimark.

WWD: What was the relationship with Trimark like?

KL: Well, they did more for that film than I think almost anyone could have done, because they really put everything into it. They pushed it. I mean they really put a lot into it. And so it was very emotional from their point of view as well. It was a gamble.

WWD: Were you surprised by the massive critical acclaim that *Eve's Bayou* received? How did you handle all the attention? Suddenly you were a triple threat: an actor, a writer, and a director.

KL: It was great, even though some of it went by in a blur, I've got to tell you. There is a part of me that wishes I could remember every moment. The first time we screened it for a real audience, we got three standing ovations. It was one of those moments in life where everything is beautiful. We all burst into tears—all the producers, all the men, everyone. It was a very, very big moment for us, with our little film.

WWD: How do you and Vondie keep your life in balance, when both of you are actors and directors, and you have children to take care of as well? That's a lot to keep on top of. How do you keep the whole thing in balance?

KL: It works pretty well. We are each other's best support, so it's like having somebody who understands immediately where you're coming from. We take turns talking about the daily battles we have to go through with work and check in with each other during the day to find out what the status is. My first thought when you asked that question was that you should have seen this past summer. It got really crazy when Vondie was directing Hunter, our son, in his new movie, *Waist Deep* (2006). That was really insane.

WWD: *The Caveman's Valentine*, which you directed in 2001, was an impressive and beautiful film, with another superb performance by Sam Jackson. But it just didn't click with the public, despite a larger budget and pretty good distribution.

KL: No, it didn't.

WWD: What do you think happened? Was the material too bleak? Or was it that people found it tough to identify with Sam's character, Romulus Ledbetter, an acclaimed concert pianist whose life has been derailed by severe mental illness?

KL: Well, I think that the script was always one of those that people either love or hate. And I think the movie kind of came out that way as well.

WWD: It was a much tougher picture to get into.

KL: Yes, it's not quite as accessible. I loved the character of Romulus and wanted to do it with Sam very badly. And I loved the script and the book (both by George Dawes Green), and I just thought it would all work out. But it was really the character that I fell in love with. And so, even though it didn't really hit, I'm glad I made it.

WWD: So how did you absorb going from heaven to purgatory, so to speak, when the film didn't hit?

KL: It was a reality check. But I think that we knew from the beginning that *Caveman's Valentine* was much, much riskier and that it really needed people that were in love with it behind it. And at a certain point there was kind of a regime change in the company that really didn't get it. So I think that, for whatever reason, it never really found its home. It's funny, because there are people out there who love it. But it never could find its way to those people who would probably be the right audience for it, and so it was genuinely hard.

WWD: Since then, you've done an episode of *ER*, "It's All In Your Head" in 2002, and you appeared in the documentary film *In the Company of Women* (2004), directed by Gini Reticker and Lesli Klainberg.

KL: Yes.

WWD: What was that like?

KL: It was great. I've done a few of those where I've been asked to talk about my work, and that was one of those projects that came out very well. But I'm never quite comfortable just talking.

WWD: About your work?

KL: About anything, actually. I don't like to verbalize too much. I think I'm better when I'm actually creating.

WWD: Do you prefer to direct, act, or write? What's your favorite part of the filmmaking process?

KL: I love directing.

WWD: You love it even more than acting now?

KL: Oh, yes. Acting was my first love, so it will always be my first love. But now I want to direct more films.

WWD: That's like Ida Lupino, the forties actress who went on to direct a bunch of very interesting movies in the fifties. Just before she died, she was asked which she preferred, acting or directing. She chose directing without hesitation.

KL: Yes, definitely, there is no contest.

WWD: Why do you think that is?

KL: You can control the entire vision, from the idea that's in your head to the finished project on the screen. And then the collaboration is so intimate. As an actor, of course, you are collaborating with the other actors and with the director, but that's still just a portion of the whole picture. There is something about the collaboration that I find deeply, deeply rewarding. When you put together a team, and everybody is there for the project, and everybody believes in it, and everybody is trying their hardest with very little money, it's magic to me. I like the collaborating. I like the people part of it. I like the sense of accomplishment you feel when you actually are able to present it.

WWD: So you get a real sense of being there in the moment with the actors, the crew, everyone?

KL: Oh, yes.

WWD: What are you working on now?

KL: Well, I'm just about to start shooting on *Talk to Me* (2007), the story of Washington, DC, radio personality Ralph "Petey" Greene, an ex-con who became a popular talk show host and community activist in the sixties. It's just an incredible, incredible story, and I feel very passionate about it. I think it's going to be a fantastic movie. Don Cheadle and Cedric the Entertainer star in it. I really think it's going to be a great film.

WWD: What are your hopes for the future of cinema? Do you see the coming digitization of cinema as something that will be positive for independent filmmakers, or does the whole thing still rest on the issue of distribution? Where do you see yourself in your career in ten years? What is the primary work that you hope to accomplish as a filmmaker?

KL: Well, I think the whole thing rests on distribution.

WWD: I would agree.

KL: I think it's great when you can get stuff into the pipeline now with the Internet; and with all these new outlets, it's hard to say what's going to happen next. I guess I would like to change audience perceptions in a way, especially the way African American films are perceived. I would like to be a major influence in opening up the spectrum, and I would like to be an influence on a new generation of filmmakers. One thing we know for sure is that the medium is going to change. But I think that there will always be a future for celluloid and dark theaters.

Distaff and Distinguished:
The New Wave of Women Directors

Sarah Kuhn / 2007

From *Backstage* magazine, vol. 48, no. 29 (July 16, 2007), pp. 12–13, 19. Reprinted by permission.

Note: The following is an abbreviated version of the original article.

There's a preconceived notion of what a Hollywood director is supposed to look like. "He's 25 to 45 and has that kind of scruffy, slightly rumpled look," says Kasi Lemmons, the filmmaker behind *Eve's Bayou*, *The Caveman's Valentine*, and the recently released *Talk to Me*. "And he's a white man." She laughs, gesturing to her flowing dreadlocks and decidedly nonscruffy appearance. "I do not fit that aesthetic."

Indeed, there are plenty of filmmakers who are worlds away from the stereotype. Female directors are making their mark in Hollywood, with films as diverse as their backgrounds. "There are a lot of us that don't fit that pattern, and we do manage to work," Lemmons says. "Hopefully, our work speaks for itself. I think if you look at my work, you see three interesting, different films—yet they're all very me."

Lemmons' path to the director's chair was, she says, "very organic." She began her career as an actor, guest-starring on series such as *Spenser: For Hire* and appearing Off-Broadway in Lanford Wilson's *Balm in Gilead*. World events inspired her to study filmmaking at New York's New School for Social Research in the late 1980s. "The war in Nicaragua was going on, and I was a very passionate and politicized person," she recalls. "I thought, 'I'm going to make documentaries, so I've got to go to film school and learn to use a camera.'"

She made a successful documentary short, *Fall from Grace*, and was hired to write a screenplay for Bill Cosby (though the project didn't make it to production). As she was gaining traction as a writer, she also began to land more acting gigs: plum roles in such high-profile projects as *The Silence of the Lambs*, *Candyman*, and *Hard Target*. Around this time she penned *Eve's Bayou*, a script focusing on a Louisiana-dwelling African American family in the 1960s. "I wrote it to have a part for myself to act when I got a little older," she says. "I thought, 'Okay, when I no longer fit in the little black dress, I'm going to play Mozelle or Roz in *Eve's Bayou*.'"

Lemmons' life, however, took a different turn. Her theatrical agent at the time, Ken Kaplan, passed the script to literary agent Frank Wuliger of the Gersh Agency. Wuliger took Lemmons on and has repped her ever since. "He and I tried to find a director to do (*Eve's Bayou*), but everybody said no," she says. "So I woke up one day with the epiphany that I should direct it myself."

To convince people that she was capable of helming the film, she made a short, *Dr. Hugo*, that served as a "pilot" for her feature and helped secure the participation of star Samuel L. Jackson. *Eve's Bayou* won the 1998 Independent Spirit Award for best first feature and earned kudos from the National Board of Review, which named it outstanding directorial debut.

Lemmons has continued to build on her reputation as a director with a distinctively poetic vision and a fondness for flawed, dynamic characters. Her latest film, *Talk to Me*, is a vibrant biopic of famed 1960s deejay Petey Greene (Don Cheadle). "(All of my movies) have a lot of similarities to me, but they're very different in feeling and in execution," she says. "I do what feels appropriate to the film I want to make. And I want to make what I want to make. That's the hardest part with me, I think. I have to be in love with a movie in order to do it."

The filmmaker believes that actors are particularly well-suited to becoming directors, but she has no current plans to return to performing. "I have a much greater appreciation for actors as a director," she says. "And in some ways I feel I can give more to the art of acting as a director—(by having) beautiful parts, (casting) wonderful actors, and really (helping) them to be as good as they possibly can be in a performance."

"Stick (with) It"

Being female in a male-dominated profession is certainly a challenge—but one Lemmons tries not to overthink. "(Directing) came very naturally to me; I never thought about my femaleness playing into it," she says. "I can be very female; *Eve's Bayou* is very feminine in some ways, but (*Talk to Me*) isn't. I feel versatile, like I can direct whatever I want to direct if I love it."

Jessica Bendinger, who made her feature directorial debut last year with the tart comedy *Stick It*, says the field is still very male-dominated, but "Hollywood is blind," she says. "They don't care whether you are white, black, male, female. They just want to make money. That's great news for anybody who is commercially minded."

Like Lemmons, Bendinger got her start in a different line of work. She fell in love with film at a young age, thanks to such classics as *The Bad News Bears* and *Diner*. After graduating from New York's Columbia University, she worked in music journalism, writing for *Spin* magazine and penning scripts for MTV News. "We used to get these electronic press kits at MTV, and we'd have to go through and decide what we were going to cover on the news," she recalls. "There was an EPK for *Say Anything* that came in, and I read that Cameron Crowe had written for *Rolling Stone* before he became a filmmaker. I suddenly went, 'Oh my God, somebody made that leap from music journalism to movies.' Suddenly it was possible."

Bendinger experienced a fair amount of struggle while trying to make it in the industry. She was rejected from the Sundance Screenwriters Lab and wrote a TV spec for *Mad About You* that garnered her some attention but no job. Finally, a friend called her with an opportunity to write for a new French series, *Sous Le Soleil*. "They wanted American writers to come and give it a real American flavor, and then they would translate the scripts," she recalls. "So I had to leave the country to get my first writing job."

Upon returning to the States, Bendinger wrote a spec screenplay that landed her a few meetings. When someone told her she should go into these meetings with an idea to pitch, she came up with the concept of a smart, snarky cheerleading movie called *Bring It On*. She pitched it twenty-eight times and got one yes—from the production company Beacon Communications. The finished film, directed by Peyton Reed and starring Kirsten Dunst, was a surprise hit.

The success of *Bring It On* allowed Bendinger to move into directing, which she'd always hoped to do. "When I was working at MTV, as writers we produced packages and stuff, so I had some experience in editing bays," she recalls. "And I had directed music videos for a couple of years. I always hoped that someday I would get to merge the visual with the page again. I was kind of biding my time, knowing if I could write the right script at the right time, given my track record with *Bring It On* and with the demographic, I could probably get a shot to direct it."

She penned *Stick It*, a fresh, funny look at the world of competitive gymnastics, with directing in mind. Because three studios were interested in the script, she was able to sell it with herself attached to direct.

Balance the Babies

One challenge specific to being a female filmmaker, Lemmons says, is trying to balance the heavy responsibilities of career and motherhood. "Being a mother is hard," she says. "That is something I decided I was going to deal with. I was pregnant when I got my green light for *Eve's Bayou*, and I had just had the baby when I directed it. So that's challenging, but it's a decision I've made, and now it's a decision I can actually talk to my children about. They're proud of me, you know?"

Danish director Susanne Bier, who received an Oscar nomination for her 2006 film *After the Wedding*, says you must firmly structure your life in order to make it work. "I spent the first years of my career using all my money on having help in the house, and I never got to save up money or buy anything, because I really purposefully used my money to work, and I also knew I wanted to have a happy life for my kids," she says. "I made a very firm decision on making those two things work."

She believes her region of the world is a bit more encouraging to female directors than Hollywood is. "In our part of the world, we have public child-care facilities," she says. "So there is a general sort of notion that women (have) professional lives and that women who (have) professional lives obviously have families and kids. I think that notion, on a deeper level, is part of determining women's futures. I think a lot of talented women in the States avoid becoming filmmakers because it would be so hard to have both (family and career)."

Bier, who has made a number of successful Scandinavian films, transitioned into directing after studying architecture. "I realized after a while that I wasn't going to sit in an architect's office and design," she says. "I became more interested in the human beings that were going to be within the walls. I got interested in set design; I slowly moved towards filmmaking while still doing architecture. At some point, I thought, 'Maybe I'll be a set designer,' but then I started reading scripts, and I realized that actually I (wanted) to become a director."

Bier recently made her first American film, *Things We Lost in the Fire*, which is scheduled to premiere this fall. The intricately crafted drama focuses on a widow (Halle Berry) who forms a bond with her late husband's troubled best friend (Benicio Del Toro). "When you are European, you have all these prejudices about American movies: that they are (made by) evil studios that are going to come and prevent you from doing what you think is right to do," she says. "In practice, it was the opposite. It's been a very exciting, very inspiring process throughout the entire film. And (DreamWorks) has not fulfilled my prejudices at all. In the script meetings, they would have comments like, 'We want it to be really honest, we want it to be edgy, we want it to be really interesting.'"

Hold Fast to Your Beliefs

These four filmmakers vary greatly when it comes to background and subject matter, but they have a few things in common. For example, they're all very passionate about the casting process. Lemmons notes that, with few exceptions, she auditions all her actors. And Bier believes it's crucial to find the perfect actor for every role, down to the smallest. "There's a lot of texture in parts which are not necessarily just the main characters," she says. "I'm extremely involved in all of that."

Manafort is so particular about casting that two of her leads in *The Beautiful Ordinary*, Lyndsy Fonseca and Shahine Ezell, weren't cast until the day before principal photography began. "I was on location watching tapes and tapes and tapes," she remembers. "And I was just refusing to cast the roles, because I hadn't found the right person. Literally, the day before (principal photography), these two tapes came in. I was really holding out for the right people, and fate took care of me. I don't know what would have happened if it didn't."

Additionally, all of these women have achieved a measure of success by staying true to themselves and their visions. "I think women are very well suited to the (directing) process if they can really balance their yin and yang and don't try to be (guys)," Bendinger says. "Be who you are. Be you."

Kasi Lemmons: *Talk to Me*

Melissa Silverstein / 2007

From *In Her Voice: Women Directors Talk Directing* by Melissa Silverstein. New York: Women and Hollywood. © 2013 by Melissa Silverstein/Women and Hollywood. Reprinted by permission of Melissa Silverstein, Founder/Publisher of Women and Hollywood.

Bio: Kasi Lemmons's first feature-length film, *Eve's Bayou*, became the highest grossing independent film of 1997. The film won the Independent Spirit Award for Best First Feature and received seven NAACP Image Award nominations, including Best Picture. In addition, Lemmons received a special first-time director award, created just for her, from the National Board of Review. She also won the Director's Achievement Award at the 9th Annual Nortel Palm Springs Film Festival.

Kasi Lemmons's feature *Talk to Me*, starring Don Cheadle, was released nationwide in July 2007 by Focus Features to widespread critical acclaim. She received the 2008 NAACP Image Award for outstanding directing.

Lemmons is developing a film adaptation of the gospel musical *Black Nativity* for Fox Searchlight. She was also awarded a fellowship by the WGA and the Franco-American Film Fund to develop her script, *Strangers in Paris*, in France as part of the Autumn Stories project.

Lemmons has worked extensively as a mentor and educator. She attended New York University School of the Arts, UCLA, and The New School of Social Research Film Program. She resides in New York City with her husband and two children.

Description: At its heart, *Talk to Me* is a love story between two men. There's nothing romantic going on between the two lead characters, D.J. Petey Green (Don Cheadle) and Dewey Hughes (Chiwetel Ejiofor), but it is a love story nonetheless. Petey is an ex-con whose only ambition is to be on the radio. It's 1966, and Washington, DC is in the throes of the Civil Rights Movement. Petey manages to harangue Dewey into a job at the radio station where he works. Petey becomes a DC star because he is in the right place at the right time. He speaks honestly and openly about his life as a Black man in a white world. Dewey has big dreams for Petey beyond the radio and their relationship unravels as he pushes him to heights he can't handle.

Interview Date: November 6, 2007

Women and Hollywood: This film is a love story between two men, which is rarely seen on film. Why was it important for you to tell this story?

Kasi Lemmons: One of the most important films for me growing up was *Butch Cassidy and the Sundance Kid*, which was a movie about male friendship. It helped shape my feelings about film relationships and I realized I didn't see that. I wanted to get inside a relationship between two men where they could be vulnerable and need each other. I feel that it's real, and yet men are very afraid of showing emotion and being demonstrative. It helps us to understand men more when we realize they are capable of these friendships.

W&H: When did you know you wanted to make the switch to the directing chair? (Previously an actress, one prominent role Lemmons played was Jodie Foster's roommate in *Silence of the Lambs*.)

KL: It happened very organically. It was the late '80s and I was into politics. I went to film school thinking I would put a camera on my shoulders and make documentaries. The first film I made was about being homeless in New York. But, I had a tendency to dramatize. Bill Cosby then hired me to write a screenplay (which was never produced) and that's how I got into the Writer's Guild.

The storyteller part of me was always very alive. I wrote plays all the time. At a certain point, I had a story I could tell from the beginning to end and I realized I had to write it down. I wrote a part that I could play when I was forty. It happened faster than that. I met an agent and he said we had to put it together and find a director. People passed on it. One day I woke up and realized that I had to direct it (*Eve's Bayou*). I didn't suddenly decide that I was a director, and even after I directed *Eve's Bayou*, I thought I was done.

W&H: It's unacceptable how few women and African American women directors there are working in film today.

KL: In every other field, there are women. There are women in high levels of politics. There are women in high levels of management at the World Bank. There are women in high levels everywhere. Why is it that there are not more women directors? It just doesn't make sense. It's a particular backward industry in this country. I can't speak for other countries because they seem better.

Storytelling is not like running the World Bank. Storytelling has a masculine and feminine side. We're dealing with humanity. As artists, women are wonderful at telling men's stories, as men have been wonderful at telling women's stories. Yet at the same time, you need the push and the pull.

You need the other side of the coin.

W&H: Why does this continue to be such a problem?

KL: It doesn't make much sense that they wouldn't be interested in women's visions. Look at television. They are always looking for women's stories to tap. I think it might have something to do with the concept of what a director is—a white man, between thirty and fifty, with the hat on backward in sneakers with a little scruff.

W&H: You lobbied for this film. Did you have to work harder to get this film?

KL: I had to get the meeting. I had to wait until they had gone through meetings with the usual suspects. I made it known that I wanted to do the movie, and then, the only moment of self-consciousness I had was before the first meeting and it wasn't just that I was a woman. I went in super prepared and super passionate and I got through that meeting.

I was halfway through my second meeting, and Mark Gordon said OK.

W&H: Is this the same Mark Gordon who produces for TV?

KL: He believes in the power of women. It's something he believes in and enjoys doing without thinking. It's not that he is making a political statement; it's just the guy he is. Mark saw my passion, heard what I had to say, and said OK.

W&H: How important is it to tell African American stories?

KL: It's very important, but there have been stories I have been attracted to that have not been African American stories.

I've written all kinds of things; however, I am attracted to characters. African American stories have such a dynamic history, and it's my people so it's special to me. I think we occupy an interesting place in American history—very violent, very strong, and triumphant—and so I am drawn to those characters. I am drawn to stories.

W&H: What advice would you give a young woman director?

KL: Find a way of telling a story that represents an aspect of you, so you can use it as a calling card to help shape your identity so someone else doesn't put you in a box. Create something or find a piece of material that is a love letter to yourself.

W&H: What are you working on next?

KL: I'm writing a pilot for Mark Gordon and CBS. I am also writing a piece for Picturehouse on the Civil Rights Movement.

6 Tips for Finding Your Creative Path from *Black Nativity* Director Kasi Lemmons

Melinda Loewenstein / 2013

From *Backstage.com*, November 27, 2013. Reprinted by permission.

Kasi Lemmons is taking a new direction in her latest film, the inspirational musical Christmas story *Black Nativity*, which hits theaters Nov. 27. The film is loosely based on the 1960s stage musical *Black Nativity* by Langston Hughes. When she was pitched the idea of writing and directing *Black Nativity* for the big screen, Lemmons says "All I remember thinking is 'Look no further. I'm the person for you. I have to direct this.'" Lemmons brings an original contemporary story to the adaptation and weaves it together with the *Black Nativity* story, all the while paying tribute to Langston Hughes.

We talked to Lemmons about her latest film and her creative journey including acting, writing, and directing.

Be Open to New Avenues.

Lemmons's journey to directing started with acting. Along the way she fell into writing, when she was hired to write a screenplay for Bill Cosby while auditioning for him. After being in Los Angeles for a while, Lemmons decided to take a pilot season off from acting to write an idea that she couldn't get out of her head— and that script became *Eve's Bayou*. When she couldn't find a director for the film, she decided to direct it herself. "It wasn't like I put it together—it was the next step of making my career. It was like it just happened to be a journey into the director's chair," says Lemmons.

Find Your Way in.

"Writing is my way in," says Lemmons, who has written many of the films she's directed. Even if she's not writing the script, she's still involved in the process.

For *Black Nativity*, she found her way into the story in the early stages of putting together the pitch. "It didn't feel like it was going to be satisfying to me to just pitch the Nativity story. I wanted to make a contemporary story that would feel very relevant and very real about the problems facing families and especially in the African American community."

Put Together the Right Team.

Before casting, there was another important aspect of the *Black Nativity* creative team to be found. Lemmons says the biggest challenge was hiring the right musician to guide the musical direction of the film. She always knew she wanted to tell the story with original songs, so the musical direction was key in making the film work. "Once I decided that I wanted to do it with Raphael (Saadiq), then it became a matter of coercing him, and stalking him, and convincing him to do the movie with me." The first song Saadiq and his songwriting partner brought Lemmons was "Test of Faith." "Then I knew I was in good hands with these people," she says.

The top-notch acting team fell into place easily. Lemmons had most of the actors in mind while writing the script (Jennifer Hudson, Tyrese Gibson). "I would have been auditioning a lot for (Langston), but Jacob (Latimore) was the first person that walked in." Even though she saw more actors after him, Lemmons says, emotionally, she knew that she was going back to him.

Rehearse.

Lemmons says her directing style varies depending on the script, but she always rehearses before shooting. "*Eve's Bayou* was very specific to me, very structured and almost choreographed. *The Caveman's Valentine* was completely different—I would let Sam (Samuel L. Jackson) go and then I would use what I thought was working and kind of step in." The rehearsals allow Lemmons to talk about and explore the characters and scenes with the actors so they understand her vision.

Work Hard.

While Lemmons acts, writes, and directs, she says directing is definitely the most challenging—mainly because of the stamina it requires. "I probably work ninety hours a week for most of the year, and when I wasn't working ninety hours I was working eighty hours," she says. "It's a very, very stressful job and in the editing room you're turning around cuts like every six hours. It's really quite a difficult job with a specific skill set that's required and so it's harder to direct."

Appreciate Everyone.

"(For *Black Nativity*) I set about quite intentionally creating (a certain) environment—an environment where everything would be comfortable and happy." She wanted to create unity and hired people that she thought would be fun to work and collaborate with. Lemmons stresses the importance of creating a positive set for a successful film. "Don't melt down. You've got to stay sane and stay cool, and be nice to your crew, and thank everyone and be grateful. Show gratitude and appreciation." This attitude doesn't just bring out good performances from the actors, it creates an inclusive environment. "You never know when your life might be saved by craft services. Everybody is miserable and cold and exhausted and all of a sudden craft services comes through with cappuccinos and brownies and they save your day from taking a terrible turn. It's not just the actors, it's every single person on the set. You literally can't do it without them."

Refashioning a Gospel Story in *Black Nativity*

Rachel Martin / 2013

The new movie is based on a play by the same name by Langston Hughes. Host Rachel Martin talks with director Kasi Lemmons about her new musical drama, Black Nativity, released last week.

Rachel Martin, Host: In 1961, at the height of the civil rights movement, Langston Hughes wrote the musical play *Black Nativity*. It featured an entirely Black cast, and it was the first play to incorporate a real gospel choir.

(Soundbite of music)
Choir: (Singing) I'm coming home for you, you think (unintelligible).

Martin: Every year, roughly a quarter million people see *Black Nativity* on stage. But this year, a new star-studded production is hitting the big screen, starring the likes of Forest Whitaker, Jennifer Hudson, and Angela Bassett. The filmmaker is Kasi Lemmons. When she was growing up, seeing *Black Nativity* was a family tradition during the holidays. The original play is an uplifting story of Jesus' birth. But *Black Nativity*, the movie, as Kasi Lemmons created it, is framed with a modern tale of economic struggle. A young single mother and her teenaged son are getting kicked out of their house.

Jacob Latimore: (as Langston) We're being evicted? I thought you were going to work something out with the bank. I thought we could win it back.
Jennifer Hudson: (as Naima) I've been trying. It's hard getting that much together.
Latimore: (as Langston) So, we've got to move?

Hudson: (as Naima) Langston.
Latimore: (as Langston) Where are we going to live, ma? Why didn't tell me?

Martin: That's Jennifer Hudson playing the role of Naima. She's out of options, so she sends her son, played by Jacob Latimore, to live with her estranged parents until she can figure out what to do next. Kasi Lemmons says she wanted to write a story that today's families could relate to, so she looked inside her own family life at the time.
Kasi Lemmons: This was 2008—we're in the height of the financial crisis. And my sister and her daughter moved in with my mom—her house was foreclosed on.

Martin: She was having financial problems?
Lemmons: She was having financial problems—everybody was. It was the country. So, I wanted to root it in right then. It's a family in conflict, a family in crisis, but at the same time I wanted you to leave *Black Nativity* with the feelings that I left the theater with when I saw the stage production.

Hudson: (as Naima) (Singing) This love in my heart is all I have left. That's not enough but it's my best . . .

Martin: And, obviously, the nativity that you grew up is a musical kind of experience. You could have kept the music circumscribed to the actual pageant, but you didn't. You made a full-on musical. How is that for you as a director, this new kind of adventure?
Lemmons: Well, it's interesting. I mean, it was the way that the story felt like it wanted to tell itself. I thought it would be cool to do some original songs in different kind of genres of music and then work our way into kind of the nativity music. It was so much fun. I mean, it was really fun. It was a little bit intimidating.

Martin: There are some people involved in this project.
Lemmons: The way I got through that vat of nerves was to really partner up with Raphael Saadiq, and the first song that he wrote is "Test of Faith," where Naima's sending her son away and she sings this beautiful song. It was really amazing.

Hudson: (as Naima) (Singing) You got my attitude, and you got your daddy's blues. Want you to see love can be faithful and true. I haven't been a saint, so I'm gonna be all be, and hope someday sooner than we think, in the meantime, I've been . . .

Martin: I mean, as we mentioned, big names—not only Jennifer Hudson—Tyrese Gibson, Mary J. Blige, Forest Whitaker. I mean, what was it like on that set?

Lemmons: It was incredible. I mean, it really, really was. You know, some of them are recording artists, are a little more green to film acting. Then I have Forest Whitaker and Angela Bassett, who are, like, you know, the king and queen of, you know, stage and screen. And yet there, you know, there was Jacob, who this was only his second movie. And it was really a wonderful opportunity and a wonderful gift to kind of be there to help break him out, you know.

Martin: And the music in this film is really lovely, incredibly powerful at some points. I understand you actually helped write some of the songs. Is that correct?

Lemmons: Yeah. I mean, I had written all the lyrics— my version of the lyrics—into the script, and then Raphael and his songwriter Taura came onboard and they transformed many of the songs. But there was one song that I'd already recorded in order to kind of convince the studio to give me a green light. So, as part of my presentation to the studio, I had shot a music video of "Hush Child," the Silent Night song.

Hudson: (as Naima) (Singing) This ain't easy. I got a mouth to feed but I can't make these ends meet. Got (unintelligible) my Lord don't hear my prayers, I've never been (unintelligible). The silence is too loud for me. Life just ain't fair. Sleep in heavenly peace. Sleep in heavenly peace.

Martin: I hope you don't mind me asking— you've said before that writing this film helped you deal with the loss of your sister. She died of breast cancer. And since then, you've taken in her teenage daughter as part of your family. The film has similar themes of loss and reimagining family, reinterpreting family in new times. Can you talk a little bit about how making this movie helped you specifically during that time?

Lemmons: Well, I was between drafts and I was at a point where I really needed to deliver the draft that was going to get the movie green-lighted. And then my sister got very sick. So, I took a break from it. And then after she passed away, I honestly—I didn't know if I was going to be able to come back to writing at all. I mean, I couldn't imagine the next step except that I had these kids and a grieving child to take care of. But this really was a great rock to hold onto for me. You know, it was very fun to write and kind of, you know, uplifting.

Martin: For people who know *Black Nativity* intimately, it's been perhaps part of their family tradition, what do you want them to walk away from this movie with?

Lemmons: Well, it's a family drama and they're dealing with the sorts of problems that are prevalent, not just in African American families but, you know, that are kind of very familiar and might have a solution that feels so unattainable and yet in some ways it's simple, calls on our deepest generosity of the soul, you know. Family estrangement is a subject that has always interested me. You know, how did they get that way and, you know, what do you do about it?

Latimore: (as Langston) (Singing) I don't know why I'm here or where I am going anymore. Mama tried to save me from the street war but . . .

Martin: Director Kasi Lemmons. Her newest film is called *Black Nativity*. Thank you so much for taking the time to talk with us.
Lemmons: Thank you for having me.

Latimore: (as Langston) (Singing) If I'm gonna get the strength again, I gotta move slow. Steady, stay ready, 'cause it's worth waiting for. Daddy (unintelligible) when I wasn't (unintelligible). It wasn't me that a (unintelligible) . . .

Third Act: The Journey of a Hollywood Director

Natalie Chang / 2016

How Kasi Lemmons found an opening in the unforgiving boardrooms of Hollywood

Kasi Lemmons wants to make sure she's getting her point across. She's eloquent and measured in her speech, and she's not afraid to take pauses to turn words over in her mind before responding to a question. Every so often, she interrupts herself to ask, "You know what I mean?" and the question isn't a placeholder. It's a genuine marker of her warmth and intelligence; it's also a gentle but clear-eyed way of making sure we're paying attention to what she has to say.

That desire to say something and to have it heard has taken her on a journey from her beginnings as a young actress to her status as an acclaimed director, a singular writer, and a teacher. She thinks of herself as a storyteller above all; she defines herself by an innate need to express herself.

Lemmons is intent on making her voice heard in an industry characterized by the height of its barriers. "I have to really, really become obsessed with a character," Lemmons says. "The spark of whatever it is kind of eats away at me until it needs to be expressed." Lemmons distinguished herself by developing the kinds of stories that Hollywood hadn't thought of yet.

Her advancement into writing and directing wasn't something she planned, but she realized, even as she was landing acting roles in movies like Spike Lee's *School Daze* and sharing the screen with Jodie Foster in *Silence of the Lambs*, that she had always channeled her creativity in more ways than one. "It *happened*," she says. "It unfolded in ways that I couldn't have predicted. Looking at it in retrospect, I can say these three things were married and this was a future that was inside of me from the beginning. I was a writer and actor, and the marriage of acting and writing was going to be directing."

For Lemmons, the progression of her career was the natural conclusion of a childhood in Boston theater, film school in New York, auditions in LA, and years of constant writing. Even if it was natural, however, the journey wasn't—and still isn't—easy. The door to show business is generally unyielding for any hopeful: For a young woman of color, the odds of breaking out into the mainstream are even slimmer.

But Lemmons didn't dwell on her odds, and instead took the barriers that rose in front of her as challenges that she could surmount, as long as she was willing to persevere. "What am I going to do to get on their list?" she remembers asking herself. "How can I convince them that I'm smarter than everybody else, and more prepared? It was motivating to me."

Being a woman of color in a field predominantly white and male came with its creative advantages, too. Lemmons knew that she had stories to tell, with unique perspectives and voices, that hadn't been brought to Hollywood yet. Her writing and directorial debut, *Eve's Bayou*, is an unsettling and beautiful story about one Louisiana family's series of revelations: It's complex, mystical, and doesn't easily lend itself to categorical definition. Critics gave *Eve's Bayou* overwhelmingly positive reviews, and the film itself, along with Kasi and its performers, were nominated for and won several independent awards. The next film she directed, *The Caveman's Valentine*, starred Samuel L. Jackson as a homeless man in New York who sets out to solve a murder, all the while battling with hallucinations and mental illness. Lemmons clearly doesn't shy away from complicated material: It's rather what she's most interested in.

"I had a big dream that I was very intent on vigorously fulfilling," Lemmons says. "That's the way I lived it: I'm an artist. I know my history, I know my roots, I know I can be an artist. Of course I'm a minority, but that makes it interesting. You know what I mean?"

But Lemmons acknowledges that no matter how interesting a story is, there are expectations in Hollywood to stay within the dominant cultural language. She remembers that scripts she wrote featuring predominantly white characters were more readily received, and that moving through Hollywood meant moving through a series of "endless boys' clubs." She found that, for the most part, the people who ruled Hollywood production were largely interested in stories with characters in whom they could see themselves: "They naturally gravitate towards each other without even thinking about it."

Lemmons believes that the lack of representation of women and people of color in film and media is something that has to be actively addressed—institutionally and on an individual level. Only six of the top five hundred box office films of all time feature a protagonist who is a woman of color; only nine percent of the top two hundred fifty domestic-grossing films of 2015 were directed by women.

"This was an evolutionary thought of mine: We have to be a little bit more aggressive and more overtly supportive of each other," Lemmons says. "We have to be more willing to say, you know what? Look at this picture, what's wrong with this picture? If you don't see it, I'm going to tell you."

And she also looks towards the future—the next generation of filmmakers and artists, many of whom she advises at Sundance, at New York University's Tisch School of the Arts, and at Film Independent. "We're all conducting our own revolution," she says. "What are we going to do about women working in the industry? My way of dealing with it is to teach."

As a teacher, she has the chance "to help participate in the education of women filmmakers and interesting filmmakers and filmmakers of color," and she describes that experience as a way for her to live in an optimistic future. "I want them to be inspired, to stay positive and focused, because that's what it takes," she says. "It's perseverance and stamina and a love and interest in the process."

Success in her industry is rare, she notes, which is why a genuine love of the artistic process is necessary to anyone embarking on a career in filmmaking. But success is subjective, and Lemmons's definition of it has evolved over the years. Fresh out of film school and going from audition to audition, she dreamed about being a mainstream name and starring in big-name box office films. Later, as she became more immersed in writing and directing, nominations and awards beckoned.

She achieved those things, ultimately, through a combination of firm dedication to self-expression and willingness to keep her hands in the process. But after Lemmons became involved with teaching, and after having children and raising a family, success came to mean something a little more abstract. "Maybe I'll never make a lot of money, but on the other hand, I've never done anything else (besides filmmaking)," she says. "Even teaching: I choose to teach, I don't need to teach. So I really live the life that I want to live, and that is success to me."

Lemmons isn't done yet. She just signed a deal to direct an adaptation of *The Other Wes Moore*, a *New York Times* best-selling biography, for HBO, and she's determined to keep writing and telling the stories that matter to her, the way she thinks they should be told.

"(These stories) are what I really want to say in a life-mission way. I still believe, more now than I did then, that I can write anything and I might write anything. You can't hold me to one subject or one culture in terms of my art," Lemmons says. "You know what I mean?"

Kasi Lemmons Interview

Christina N. Baker / 2017

From *Contemporary Black Women Filmmakers and the Art of Resistance* by Christina N. Baker. Columbus: The Ohio State University Press. © 2018. Reprinted by permission.

Christina Baker: Since you've been in the situation of writing, directing, and acting, how has each experience been different for you? I'm really interested in your sense of having creative control.

Kasi Lemmons: Well, there's a relationship between acting, writing, and directing. I kind of feel like directing is some sort of child of writing and acting. And, there's a relationship between the three, but, they're very, very different. When I was acting—I had a great, great joy in acting. All the jobs I did, I would have done for free. I liked it. It was my first love. I thought it would never grow old. But, I was, kind of, unfulfilled. And, of course, I didn't have any creative control, really. I had a little bit of control over my performance, when I did.

Acting's very elusive, and difficult, and worthy of pursuing, because you never get as great at it as you want to be. But, there's nothing like the feeling of something coming from your imagination, and getting onto screen. That's a completely different exercise, actually, and a very different art form. And, for me, when I'm writing and directing, I get to act, as well. I get to work that muscle out, somehow, through the performances of the actors. And, I'm completely in awe of actors. I love actors, and I love them even more as a director than I did when I was acting.

And somehow, that transmutation, and that alchemy of bringing performances to life in words that you've written, and then, seeing the final product onscreen. And, getting the entire orchestration. Directing is more than directing actors—it's everything. It's everything that you see, and everything that you hear, is orchestrated, and involves a very intense collaboration with many, many people who help bring your vision to fruition. And, it's a very different feeling. It's almost like, playing a really good violin solo, versus conducting an orchestra, with a composition you've written. That's an amazing feeling.

Baker: It sounds like it would be a great experience.

Lemmons: Yeah. So, the most artistically fulfilling experiences I've had have been directing. Definitely, directing. Writing/directing is a beautiful thing when you come at a project from zero, and try and capture it. But, honestly, I've had very fulfilling experiences on things that I was involved with—but, I didn't originate the material—I've had very fulfilling experiences on those films, as well. Because there is a lot of creative control, as a director. Of course, it's the collaboration, it's for an audience, and it's financed by other people, and it involves a lot of negotiation. But, at the same time, it's where I felt the most artistically fulfilled.

And, more than that, it's where I feel I have something to give. There are a lot of good actors. And even though, right now, there are a lot of great women directors working. It's still a place where I feel that I'm definitely needed.

Baker: You mentioned this collaboration. Do you feel that there have been times when your creative vision as a writer or a director has not been fully realized because of this, perhaps, collaboration or compromise, maybe? Do you feel like you've had to compromise in your work, at times?

Lemmons: Oh, yeah, we all do. I don't know that you would find anyone who says, "I haven't had to compromise." Maybe, if they finance their films them-selves. Usually, we have to compromise. And, there've been a couple of times where I felt compromised—I felt that the work was compromised. Not that often, really, not that often, I've gotta say. But, definitely, once; definitely, it's happened. And, in some ways, I think that that's part of it. If you had asked me at the time, it was, kind of, the worst thing. It wasn't great. It hurt. But now, I've become more philosophical, and it's like, "Well, these things happen." If you talk to people that have made a lot of movies, they can, just, cite all kinds of experiences. It's like, "Oh, well that wasn't as good an experience as this was."

If you talk to somebody like Mira Nair, she just worked, and worked, and worked, and worked. I am just completely in awe of her. And, she's somebody that I admire greatly. I've had a chance to interview her, in a very long interview. And, just listening to her talk—it's a storied career. Some experiences are good experiences, some experiences are bad experiences. Sometimes, your artistic vision is fully realized; sometimes, it's compromised. And so, what do you learn from it? And, what do you learn that you're able to bring forward into what you do next? And, honestly, being in show business, I think, so much of the key is, just, not being squashed. Like, getting up. Like, you, just, get up. And, really, it's part of the journey, and part of the trick to it, like, "last man standing wins." You just keep going. If this is what you do, then, just keep going.

Baker: Is there a particular experience when you, on the one hand, you felt like you were able to get your vision, or, what you really wanted to come to fruition happen, compared to a time when you did feel like you had to do a little more of the compromising? Are there two experiences that you could, perhaps, compare or contrast?

Lemmons: You know, I could, but I'd rather keep the weight on myself. Because, in some ways, if there are mistakes that—in some ways, I have to look at my own part in it—and, I think if I start talking about things where I had to compromise, I would start to, perhaps, involve other people. It's unnecessary. Certainly *Eve's Bayou* is a place where, I felt that, very close to one hundred percent of what I wanted got on the screen—very, very close.

And, even though there were some big fights, and there were definitely compromises made, it came very close to being the movie that was in my head, and, that was, kind of, a magical experience. And, I've gotta say, *Talk to Me* was the same way. Even though I didn't originate the material, I felt that the movie that I fell in love with was the movie that I made. And, I loved it after I made it. It's like, "Wow, I love this movie!" Every time I'm watching, I'm like, "Wow, I love this movie!" But, in some ways, *Talk to Me* and *Eve's Bayou* are movies that at this point now, with some distance—it takes me a while to be able to watch my own work—but, at this point now, I really can watch with relish, just enjoy. I can say, "Wow! I really love this sequence! I really love this moment." And so, those are the films where I feel that I've been the most artistically successful, for a number of reasons. And, films where I felt that I've been less artistically successful, I'd rather just, focus on my own part in it. But those are the films that I feel that, for a number of reasons, I got the support, and had the vision, and had extraordinary collaborators, everybody working towards the same goals. And, yeah, so, those are the ones. But, honestly, in terms of the experience, they're all different.

In terms of the experience of just filming something—*Black Nativity* was a wonderful shoot. It was stressful, but, we liked making the movie. It had a lot of joy in the shooting of it. There was all this art, there were these beautiful dancers. So, it was very, very fun to shoot.

Baker: And, I appreciate and I think it's a difficult thing for most people to do, as far as taking responsibility for everything that you do. When you advise students, or when you teach your courses, do you use as examples your experiences from *Eve's Bayou* and *Talk to Me*, and the positive things that you took from those experiences?

Lemmons: Well, I'm very, *very* candid with my students. So, I will definitely tell them what, exactly, I think went wrong, and what, exactly, I think went right, and for what reasons, because I think it's important for them to learn those things.

And, I'm philosophical, because it pays to be. So, if I have a difficult relationship, I talk to them about it, because they need to know that there are difficult relationships. So, one thing I try to tell them is, never call anybody a "motherfucker" because life is long, and, you just never know who you're gonna work with again. And so, I tell them, "Try not to curse anybody out," because, even in the most painful situations that I've been in, professionally, I could have dinner with that person, and be perfectly civilized. And so, it's learning when it's appropriate to be explosive, and when—which is, most of the time, I'd say—it's, just to be cool. Roll with the punches. Sleep on important decisions, and, try and treat everybody with respect, while, of course, giving the ultimate respect to your project.

That's the hard thing, how protective are you? And, of course, the big trick of it is, that they hire directors to be protective. So, they want us to prevent them from destroying the work. In some ways, they want you to protect your own work. If you're a pushover, nobody wants to work with you. Or, if you get lost, your compass is not true north, and you can get thrown off balance easily, nobody wants to work with a director like that. They want you to have backbone, and protect your work. But, it's a fine line, there's many lines, and, you have to keep negotiating them, in terms of how much you protect, and how much you bend, and that's the tricky thing. And it actually requires a certain skill set, and a certain personality, frankly.

Baker: Is that something that you feel that you developed, over the years?
Lemmons: Yeah, definitely, as a director, I developed it. And, my entire world view, in terms of directing, did change. I predicted I would be a professor at some point in my life. I'd be a very popular professor. So, that's the part of my life that I can predict. So much has happened, that I could never predict. When I finished *Eve's Bayou*, I was like, I did not know that I needed to direct again. It's like, "Well, there. I've done it." That was great for me, personally. Just a good experience, and, "Wow!" It was like—I don't know—great sex, or something, it's like, "Okay!" And then, you may get that nagging, like, "Wait a minute, I'm satisfied, but I'm not done! Because, that felt so good, maybe I can do it again!" You can chase that high. But that took a minute.

There was a period of time, where I had finished *Eve's Bayou*, and I was like, "Okay, I don't know what I'm gonna do now, I don't know if I'm gonna write a novel, I don't know if I'm gonna go back to acting. I don't know what I'm gonna do, but I got that off my chest." So, I didn't really predict that I would need to keep going in the way that I have needed to keep going. I knew I was a writer, and by the time I made the movie, I'd become a professional writer, but I didn't really understand the depth at which writing would be so necessary, and that I would get to express this many things. Because I write constantly. The odds of what you write going into production, it's very tricky odds. But I've written many, many, many, many things. And, that has been very sustaining—in a weird way, it's been kind of punishing, too—but it's been very sustaining, artistically, because I'm always creating.

Baker: Do you feel that some sense of community in your field, or that a support system, has been really important for you to keep going, to keep that motivation to keep writing, and directing new projects?
Lemmons: Yeah, absolutely.

Baker: Where is that support system for you?
Lemmons: It's kind of where it's always been; it's my friends, my husband. My husband's a big support system. I don't know that I could do what I've done if I wasn't married to somebody who's supportive. So, that's been incredibly important. And then, my friends . . . my friends that are in show business, and my friends that aren't—because, sometimes, you don't want to talk about it—and, that still can be supportive. But I do have friends in the industry that are a support system to me. And my editor is a huge support system. Some directors that are friends of mine. And, in a way—this may be an answer to a different question— but, in some ways, even my students are supportive. Because, in talking about their work—I don't know, I can't explain—in ways that are hard to explain, it bolsters me. And, in helping them figure stuff out, and helping them navigate it, and being there for them, it's also supporting me. Everybody that does it, knows it, but it's hard to articulate how that happens, but it definitely happens.

Baker: I understand.
Lemmons: It definitely happens. Right? You're a teacher.

Baker: Yeah, I can understand, what you're saying there. And would you say that women, or students of color, or African American students, have been the ones who have been more likely to look to you for support? I'm curious if that identification, racially, or as far as gender, has been something that you think has been an important part of that support?
Lemmons: Yeah, I do. Particularly Black students. But, honestly, ethnic, Indian students, gay students—the kids that gravitate to me are not, necessarily, the straight, white men. But I get them, too. But I do feel that the students of color and the women need me. They need me, by example. And, they also need me, specifically. And so, that's been very important to me, and also incredibly fulfilling for me, in terms of the artists that I'm helping to support. It's gratifying because you feel like you're changing the world, you're changing the landscape.

Baker: Okay, yeah, there are so few women, and, certainly, women of color, that have been able to get to the point where you are.

Lemmons: I've had some fabulous women—I'm surrounded by them—that are amazingly talented, women that I mentor. You'll hear from them soon. When I hire an assistant, they're not, necessarily, former students, but, when I hire an assistant, I like them to be inspired filmmakers, because I feel like I can have the most impact, and it makes it interesting for me. So, if I can help mentor them while they're working with me, that makes it interesting for me. And so, all of the women that I've had assist me, or work with my company, are women that I'm interested in mentoring. They've all done amazing things. They're really starting their careers. It's great.

Baker: Have the people that you have worked closely with all been women?

Lemmons: I've had two wonderful men that have worked with me, that I loved. But, recently, yes, they've been women of color. And, there was a woman that I mentored, and she was my assistant. She was my assistant when we made *Talk to Me*. And, she was, in some ways, the first person that I, really, began to have this kind of a relationship with. And, she's somebody that I admired, somebody whose work, I thought, was very strong. And, she's actually the writer/producer of the Madam C. J. Walker (miniseries). So, I'm actually working for her now. So that, to me, is gratifying.

Baker: That's wonderful. I'm sure that's great to see. And, again, as you said, I'm not, exactly, in the same position as you, but I work with students; it's so fulfilling to see them move on, and to see how they've been successful in various ways. The line isn't as straightforward in the subject that I teach, but for you, I imagine you get a lot of fulfillment out of seeing your students move on, and write and direct.

Lemmons: I really do, yeah.

Baker: I'd like to ask about *Eve's Bayou*, specifically. You did talk about it, a little bit, in general. Can you say a little bit about how your own experiences growing up, or with your family, inspired the characters, and the development of *Eve's Bayou*?

Lemmons: Yeah, I wanted to talk about a few things. How glamorous my parents looked to me. And, in fact, they were. If I look at old pictures of my parents, they look like movie stars. They were very, very beautiful people. And their friends, they were very, very glamorous. And, I wanted to explore a way of speaking that felt very Southern, and felt like my family. And, even the way of talking to children that had a poetry to it, that could be harsh—but, it also had a love, behind it, and a poetry to it. So, those were issues and themes that I wanted to explore. And then, it developed very organically around a few characters.

I went to an audition, and the casting director, instead of reading me, he said, "Tell me a story about your family." And, I started to talk about my aunt. She was this very extraordinary character. I could do five movies on her. She was very colorful. She was kind of psychic, and she was very dramatic, and she was very beautiful, and, she had five husbands, and she was this character. Really. And I said that one day my mother—my mother and my father's sister were very close back in the day, when she was married to my father—and, one day they went to a fair together, and a fortune teller looked at my aunt's hand and said, "Some things are better left unsaid." And then, she told my aunt that all of her husbands would die. And, to my mother, I said, "Well, what did she say to you?" And, she said, "I don't know, something very normal, but I can't really remember." But Muriel was very upset—Muriel, that was my aunt's name, was very upset. And so, I told that story. And that, kind of, became Mozelle. Mozelle became an even more fantastical version of my aunt. But, honestly, my aunt was kind of fantastical.

Baker: It sounds like it.

Lemmons: When people look for autobiography in *Eve's Bayou*, the craziest character is actually somebody I drew directly from a relative of mine. And then, a lot of the banter, and the closeness between Eve and Cisely was me and my sister, for sure. Even the way that they spoke to each other, and just doing Shakespeare—like my sister and I used to read Shakespeare together. We were very close, and, we were entrusted with each other's secrets in complicated ways. Holding on to a secret can be a very big thing, and, it shaped me. My sister's secrets shaped me, in a way. And so, that's something that ended up in the movie.

But, really, I wrote a series of short stories, and then, I rolled the short stories together; and, that became *Eve's Bayou*. Around the character of Louis Batiste, who, in some ways was my father, but in many ways, wasn't my father. And, he was a character that I liked very much, and was interested in exploring a "sympathetic cad." Basically, somebody who's a very flawed man, who was also heroic to me, in a way. He was my hero in many ways. Of course, Eve is the hero, and the protagonist. But, she's a child trying to navigate an adult world to the best of her ability, at the moment.

Baker: How did you decide to incorporate the Gran Mere character?

Lemmons: I was terrified of one of my grandmothers. I had a very interesting relationship with my grandmothers. They were very different from each other. I loved them both, but I was much, much closer to one. The other one, I perceived, as, kind of, eternally cranky. And, Gran Mere is a little bit of both, but she was my father's cranky mother.

Baker: How did you envision Louis's death impacting Roz?
Lemmons: It's just as it was predicted. She will be happy again in three years.

Eve's Bayou Screenwriter Kasi Lemmons Says Black Women Writers Have a Responsibility

Joi-Marie McKenzie / 2019

From *Essence* magazine, February 5, 2019. Reprinted by permission.

Kasi Lemmons wrote *Eve's Bayou*. So she doesn't need much of an introduction, but we'll give her one anyway.

Although she's known in Hollywood as a filmmaker, Lemmons considers herself first, and always, a writer. Having discovered the art form when she was a kid, the St. Louis native had already written her first "novel" by age twelve.

Lemmons often picks titles that best suit her. In fact, she was born Karen Lemmons and went by many family nicknames as a young girl—Red, Skeeter, and even Katie. But it was the nickname her sister bestowed upon her, Kasi, that she hand-selected.

"That's the one that I took," Lemmons told *Essence* last week.

The screenwriter has been hard at work, directing the very first biopic of Black liberator Harriet Tubman. Based on a screenplay Lemmons penned with Gregory Allen Howard, Harriet will star Cynthia Erivo as the titular character along with Janelle Monae, Leslie Odom Jr., Joe Alwyn, and Jennifer Nettles.

"I can't wait for you to see it. I can't wait for people to see it," she said. "I am really excited and just tremendously honored to be bringing this story to the world. It's about time. Right?'"

Lemmons said her film will follow Tubman as she escaped from enslavement and will detail her life "until the brink of Civil War."

But a project she birthed more than twenty years ago is getting the Oscar treatment from the Academy of Motion Picture Arts and Sciences. *Eve's Bayou* is being honored with a special screening hosted by The Academy this Saturday at the Metrograph in New York.

Essence caught up with Lemmons ahead of her screening, and while she took a break from *Harriet*, to talk about writing, her mission statement as a writer and her iconic 1997 film, *Eve's Bayou*.

Essence: When did you know that you were a writer?

Kasi Lemmons: I would say knowing I was a writer, *really* feeling like I was a writer, happened in my twenties. I would write scenes sometimes in my acting class, and the acting teacher would always ask, 'Who wrote this?' And I became known for writing these contextless scenes. Then when I went to film school, and I had this little short film that I had made, and I brought it to Mr. (Bill) Cosby, who I was auditioning for with *The Cosby Show*, and . . . he said, 'What I really need is a writer.' And I said, 'I'm a writer,' and that was the first time that I actually said I'm a writer.

Essence: Wow. That's such an awesome story. What did it feel like to finally say those words? And you're not just saying them to anybody, but Bill Cosby. Despite what's happened to him now, but back then, he was a gatekeeper.

Lemmons: It was huge. He was huge. And then he gave me a homework assignment—write a scene—and he told me some basic parameters: like it's a married couple, one wants to have a kid, one doesn't. And I went home and wrote the scene, and because I was used to writing scenes that's what I did. I brought it back and that's how I got hired. And really, that was the moment.

Essence: Do you feel like writing is your calling, or is it something that you just happened upon?

Lemmons: It's my calling and the only reason that I think it's my calling is because I call myself a writer. Now when people ask me (what I do) sometimes I say I'm a filmmaker, because that seems to more adequately describe that. But I really feel like a writer. My approach to filmmaking is writing.

Essence: What did you always want to say with your writing? Did you have a mission statement for it, or is it just whatever comes to you?

Lemmons: It's whatever comes to me, but at a certain point I realized—and it became my mission, because it was also just inherently true—that all of my art is protest art. It was protesting against something and it didn't matter if the reader or the audience knew exactly what I was protesting against, but there was always a form of protest art. I felt that me, myself as an artist, this Black woman artist, was already a statement.

Essence: That actually leads me perfectly to my next question, which is do you consider yourself a Black woman in Hollywood, or a woman who happens to be Black, working in Hollywood?

Lemmons: I consider myself a Black woman in Hollywood. But I've been a Black woman all my life; I don't overly think it. You just wake up and you are. And you go on.

Essence: Your films, like *Eve's Bayou*, really tell a Black woman's story; a Black girl's story. What do you think the responsibility is for Black women writers? We do have one, whether we want it or not.

Lemmons: I agree and disagree. Like I said, just waking up every day and creating . . . that's my responsibility. Inherently my writing is political. Inherently I'm political, just by being and creating. So our responsibility to me is just to keep working. Our responsibility is to not give up. Our responsibility is to maybe try harder than everybody else. Our responsibility is to persevere and to keep creating—and from a place of honesty. Not meaning that everything you write has to be true, but has to have a truth and a truth that is inherent to us.

Essence: How did the *Eve's Bayou* story come to you?

Lemmons: At the time I was still contemplating becoming a novelist, and I'd written a series of short stories, and they all took place in this area. And it was about these kids, a little brother and sister, and then at one point I wrote the legends of the place, and how it came to be called *Eve's Bayou*. So I started writing it as a novel, and I could tell the whole story from beginning to end visually . . . but it was very difficult to get it down in a novelistic form, probably because I'm not a novel writer. It started to write itself as a screenplay. It started to come out of me, and I was like, "Oh, this is a movie scene." And so I decided to write it as a screenplay.

Essence: Do you think if the film were released this year, would it resonate differently on some notes or some lines; some scenes?

Lemmons: That's a very interesting thought. I really wonder what would happen if it were released today. I don't know. At the time, it was definitely a rare animal. It's kind of this unicorn thing. I think people didn't know how to respond to it. In the state of Black art films, there was Spike (Lee), who of course rocked the world, really rocked the world, and really changed cinema, changed Black cinema. But still I think it was weird. People didn't know what to make of this. When I was shopping the film people said, 'Well, why aren't there any white people in it? Don't you need some racist characters?' And I said, 'No.' That's what's radical about it to me—they're living in a Black world, but they could be anybody's family.

Essence: That's such interesting feedback. That's super weird to me—that you would need this antagonistic white person in this or any Black story, which we obviously know is not true.

Lemmons: Right. And I got the comment more than a few times, and I came to become more and more adamantly, militantly that this was a Black world, and all the extras were Black. It was a fable, obviously, but it took place in an American town in the South. Where there was so much intermarriage, starting from the original fable of John Paul Batiste. Of course (racism) was out there, but . . . it didn't affect their daily lives. They had some problems, complicated problems, to deal with like everyone else. Our hopes and dreams are the same as anyone else's, and we don't sit around the dinner table talking about The Man.

This interview has been condensed for clarity.

Black Feminist in Public: Kasi Lemmons on Telling Harriet Tubman's Freedom Story

Janell Hobson / 2019

From *Ms.* magazine, March 8, 2019. Reprinted by permission.

Kasi Lemmons had already made her mark in Hollywood as an actor before her directorial debut in 1997 with the critically-acclaimed *Eve's Bayou*—appearing in iconic films like *School Daze* (1988), *The Silence of the Lambs* (1991), *Candyman* (1992), and *Hard Target* (1993). In the years since, she continued shaping stories as a director: in 2001, with *The Caveman's Valentine*; in 2007, with *Talk to Me*; in 2013, with *Black Nativity*; and in episodes from the television shows *Shots Fired* and *Luke Cage*.

This year, the African American writer, actor, and producer, who is now also an Associate Arts Professor at New York University, has much to celebrate—and is breaking all new ground. *Eve's Bayou* was recently added to the Library of Congress's National Film Registry, and later this year, *Harriet*, her film about famed abolitionist and freedom fighter Harriet Tubman, is set to premiere.

Harriet Tubman passed away over one hundred years ago this weekend—on March 10, 1913. To mark the anniversary, Lemmons talked to *Ms.* about *Harriet*, freedom stories, and Black cinema.

Q: How did you come to direct this latest film on Harriet Tubman?
A: I got called in for what I thought was a general meeting with the producers about rewriting the script that they had for the Harriet Tubman movie. I definitely was interested, but I said, "Well, you know, of course it would be much more interesting if I was writing and directing," and that's when it really hit me that, Oh, I was in a meeting to talk about just that! I rewrote the script they had by Gregory Allen.

Q: What changes did you make for the film?
A: I stuck much more closely to the real Harriet Tubman story and tried to put in both lore and as many historical facts as I could. I put in as much historical language as I could.

Q: While making this film, what most inspired you about the life of Harriet Tubman?
A: There are so many things. I was most inspired by the fact that she was a mystic. That really speaks to me. That was something just really, really interesting that most people didn't know. You really can't do the Harriet Tubman story and ignore the mysticism and the visions.

Q: I can imagine how much you can visually explore with that as a filmmaker.
A: Yes. Exactly. The mysticism is something that I enjoy. It's kind of an obsession of mine, where reality ends and the mystical, more metaphysical world begins. It's so tied to her character, and she so believed it. She believed that she was in direct conversation with a higher power and that she was guided. Honestly, there are so many things about her that are inspirational. I was also inspired by the fact that she was so tiny. She was a very, very petite person and a very strong person. Early on, I read a quote when I was doing the research. There are many quotes—real quotes as opposed to fake quotes—that inspired me, but one thing she said was, "I prayed to God to make me strong enough to fight, and that's what I prayed for ever since." I thought that was an amazing thing for a woman of her time to say. She was a warrior. So, I was also inspired by her very real strengths and the fact that she was a warrior.

Q: Your comments remind me of something I read about *Harriet*'s star Cynthia Erivo, who talked about how excited she was that she too was small like Harriet Tubman. I do want to talk briefly about the controversy with the casting of Erivo because she's not a US-born Black woman. What do you think of this idea that Harriet Tubman, as a quintessential African American woman, should be played by an African American actress?
A: I understand and respect the conversation. It just doesn't have anything to do with my experience, you know what I mean? (Cynthia Erivo) was attached for years before I came onto the project. But I met her, and I said, "This woman is absolutely right for the part." I thought, she's West African, good. So is Harriet Tubman. She's petite, she's powerful, she's an athlete, she's a singer, as was Harriet. *And* she's a magnificent actress. There's nothing wrong with this picture. She's perfect for the part. More than that, when I talk to my students about directing actors and casting actors, I say, "Make sure you believe it," and she made me

believe it every day. So, her performance is flawless, and she absolutely embodies the character. Those kinds of things become much more important because when we make films, of course we're making them in a moment in time, but we're not making them *for* a moment in time. You're making something that you want to endure, that you want people to see for years to come. This petite, powerful, Black woman is playing a petite, powerful, Black woman, both of them with recent ancestors from West Africa. I have absolute faith in her, absolute belief in her. She transforms. She doesn't sound like Cynthia, she doesn't look like Cynthia. She's Harriet Tubman.

Q: What does it mean to embody someone like Harriet Tubman, who sometimes exists in our imaginations as this larger-than-life almost action superhero? How do you capture her humanity?

A: Well, that was part of the trick, and it was part of the trick of the writing because she overcame and probably was, in some ways, fueled by heartbreak, terrible heartbreak, but she was motivated by love and love of family and things that are very easy to understand and respect and to empathize with because it's part of all of our stories. We love our family. We want the best for our family. So, that's another thing that really inspired me about the story. This woman did not set out to be a hero. She set out to save herself, to free herself and then to free her family—and in the process of that, she became somebody who saved her people.

Q: Her story is then one that starts from the ordinary and enters into the heroic.

A: Absolutely. I think it's completely an inspirational story and very inspiring for women, particularly, that this little woman in this time, who could not read or write, was able to be so heroic, and really, it's about how love can inspire us to heroism. Love can be the fuel.

Q: Yes. Of course. And although she didn't read or write, she was literate in other ways.

A: She was spiritually literate. She was in a conversation that other people don't necessarily engage in.

Q: Thinking of spiritual literacy brings me back to your earlier comment about Harriet Tubman being a mystic. It also recalls for me your first film *Eve's Bayou* and the way you also engage in a mystical landscape with that film and with mystical characters. How would that film from twenty-two years ago be received if it had debuted today?

A: It's so hard for me to imagine. *Eve's Bayou* was the first screenplay that I tried to write by myself, and I wanted to write a personal story, not an autobiographical story, but something personal that was a fable because I loved fables, and I loved a certain type of magical realism in writing. I read a lot of Gabriel García Márquez and Toni Morrison, and I was very interested in that type of storytelling. And so I was interested in telling the story that existed on a very concrete and physical level, but also had a metaphysical element that was extremely intertwined and that explored issues of memory and family and secrets. I was very into Southern Gothic literature and so I wanted to make a Southern Gothic movie.

Q: Your film is such an important part of Black cinematic history, and now we are experiencing what some have called a Black cinematic renaissance with films by Barry Jenkins, Jordan Peele, Amma Asante, Steve McQueen, Boots Riley and the juggernaut that is Ryan Coogler's *Black Panther*. How does *Harriet* fit into this renaissance?
A: I'm so glad I have a film coming out in this moment, you know? Otherwise, I think I'd be envious. But at the same time, it's my fifth film, and I'm just continuing to make films. So, I'm happy to be part of all the people that are working. It's very funny when you're casting a film, and you realize every Black actor is working, and you're like, "Whoa, that's amazing!" What an amazing time. All these people are busy. This is great.

Q: And this is a totally different experience when *Eve's Bayou* debuted twenty-two years ago?
A: Yes. Absolutely. Absolutely. The question is, "Is this a moment, or is this the future?" That's something that's always hard to gauge. Maybe we're there now. Certainly, the box office potential is there, the demographic support is there. Filmmaking should reflect our times. It should reflect who we are right now. It can't be dictated to us by one group of people.

Q: When you talk about this moment, and let's hope it is the future and not just a moment, it makes me think of another time when there seemed to be a number of slavery films, or films revisiting our history, to the point that some on social media complained that they didn't want to see "another slavery movie." How do you do a film like *Harriet* and transcend audience expectations that this will be another *12 Years a Slave* or *Django Unchained*?
A: Harriet Tubman's story is not about slavery. It's about escaping from slavery. It's about freedom. Most of her story exists in freedom. So, it's a freedom story.

Q: I asked the question because sometimes there's this tendency to reduce a whole movie to slavery.

A: Well, look, we have a strong reaction to our own vile and complicated history in this country. That's a process, but bringing it to the light is part of our healing. Besides, how many films have been made about the Holocaust or World War II or about Iraq or Vietnam? We keep examining complex situations because they're interesting. That's where the conflict is, but in this country, it's extremely important for us to really examine, as artists, as historians, as journalists, as writers, to really examine our history because it's recent history, and it's very complicated history. Running away from it is extremely dangerous. Moreover, there actually have not been that many slavery movies. It's just a subject that is very upsetting and complicated.

Q: I do love what you said. That *Harriet* is not a slavery movie, it's a freedom movie.

A: It's a freedom movie.

Q: Is it also a Black feminist film?

A: Absolutely. It has to be. I don't understand how you could really be living in these times and be a Black woman and not be a Black feminist. And Harriet Tubman actually worked hard on feminist issues. That's what she did after the Civil War. So, she was a true feminist. Look, we are living in a world where we're just beginning to reckon with many of the sins of our past, and obviously, I'm talking about the #MeToo Movement as well. So, we have to be feminists. We have to remind people, "Hello. We're half of all humans." It makes no sense to oppress women. That makes no sense at all.

Director Kasi Lemmons on the Defining Moment in *Harriet*

Peppur Chambers / 2019

From *BlackGirlNerds.com*, October 28, 2019. Reprinted by permission.

Harriet is a heroic tale about American freedom fighter Harriet Tubman, who escaped from slavery only to help many others do the same as she became instrumental in changing the course of history.

Full of adventure, love, and courage, *Harriet* (written by Gregory Allen Howard and Kasi Lemmons) is sure to become an iconic film about an iconic woman (played by Cynthia Erivo), directed by an equally iconic woman, Kasi Lemmons. We sat down with Lemmons at the Toronto International Film Festival (TIFF) to talk about this wonderful film she helmed to greatness.

We were curious about everything from the nuanced, layered depictions of Black folks throughout the film in different stages of life from slavery to freedom, to Lemmons working with a cast of newcomers, including powerhouse singers and actors, and beautiful moments she experienced in the film.

Harriet goes on a journey, clearly, and meets many different people as she experiences freedom. It is important to show that people were having these different lives, which was done beautifully. There will be moments in the film where audiences may interpret scenes of freedom as a modern-day privilege and access afforded to only some Black folk; like between Marie (played by Janelle Monáe) and Harriet.

Q: How did you work through this, how did this process inform you?
A: It was very effortless. One moment that I love is this wonderful friendship between Harriet and Marie—Marie is a free woman, and a very beautiful woman, and a very composed and centered woman, and I love the moment where Marie says, "You stink," and Harriet responds, "You've never had the stink of fear." I love the empathy in Marie. "You're right, Harriet," she says, and

she apologizes. That moment is something I wrote in the script, and it became very important to me.

Q: Can you identify or describe what your leadership style is and what it was like on set?
A: What I aim to be is intense, but zen and cheerful. As an actor, I go to work with directors that I love, and I got to take different pieces that I love and say, "That's how I want to be." I worked with the late, great, Jonathan Demme; he was excited, present, intense, and cheerful and zen. All of those things. And when I worked with him, I thought if I ever direct, that's just how I want to be. The vibe on a movie comes from the top down, so I try to create a very safe environment and a kind of upbeat world. We're in this together; we're doing this together.

Q: It must have been beautiful being able to lead all of these people, to work with family and having newcomers like Jennifer, and as well as having Joe who was new to the story. What was that like?
A: We talked a lot about character. I had backstories for all of them, and we talked a lot about the history. The cast all came to us hungry. Joe came to this hungry. He was asking, "What should I read? What documentary should I see?" I said, "Ken Burns's Civil War." I could steer them in that way. I'm a writer, so to me, they're all—even the terrible ones—they're all interesting and human. I tried to be humane to all of them.

Q: Did you have a lot of time with them one-on-one?
A: We had a lot of time in terms of talking about it in preparation, and we had some rehearsal. Most of the major scenes and major characters we rehearsed—Joe and Cynthia, Jennifer, Clarke, we definitely rehearsed.

Q: What was the one defining moment for you in the film?
A: Oh my god, there were so many. But one incredible day was Harriet's walk into freedom. It was just incredible. As a director, your job is to plan things out, so I knew exactly what I wanted to shoot and what time of day I wanted to shoot exactly. We were going to shoot at sunset and play it for sunrise for her walk into freedom. We found a great hill. We had it all planned out except that we came to work that day and it was pouring.

It was miserable pouring rain, a dreary, ugly, gross day. Time was getting away from us, and we were starting to think we weren't going to get the shot. And that maybe we shouldn't get it. No, (I said), we're going to go to the top of the hill. The sky was black. I was rushing hair and makeup to get Cynthia, to get the crane built, and to get her through hair and makeup.

Cynthia came at the exact moment the crane was being built, and, at that moment, the sky cleared, the sun shone through. It was the most amazing sunset you've ever seen. In one take she walked on through to freedom. It was a magic moment. There was a double rainbow behind us. Everyone burst into tears. It was one of the most amazing moments I've ever had filming.

Kasi Lemmons: *Harriet* Is 'a Savior Movie and Not a Slavery Movie'

Daniel Joyaux / 2019

From *MovieMaker.com*, November 5, 2019. Reprinted by permission.

Kasi Lemmons didn't want her new film *Harriet* to focus on the physical violence of slavery. She wanted it to focus on the woman who freed people from it.

"If I ask you, 'What is the story of Harriet Tubman,' what are you going to say?" Lemmons said. "The story to me is about freedom, it's about movement, it's that she escaped. She escaped slavery and then she went back to liberate others. Escaping and liberating others. I really concentrated on it being a savior movie and not a slavery movie."

Despite being one of the greatest heroes of American history, Harriet Tubman has never received the biopic she deserves. Lemmons set out to correct that with *Harriet*, which stars Cynthia Erivo (*Widows, Bad Times at the El Royale*) in the title role.

After starting out as an actress in the late 1980s (her roles included playing Ardelia Mapp in Best Picture winner *Silence of the Lambs*), Lemmons went on to write and direct 1997's *Eve's Bayou*, which launched her career as a writer and director.

Around the time *Eve's Bayou* was released, screenwriter Gregory Allen Howard finished a screenplay that would become *Harriet*—after two long decades.

Lemmons talked to *MovieMaker* about the film's long journey to the screen, why Hollywood is finally ready to tell the story of a Black heroine, and how she crafted the film to make sure "a sophisticated ten-year-old could see with his grandmother."

Daniel Joyaux, MovieMakerMagazine: Harriet Tubman is a massive historical figure. Why do you think she hadn't gotten the biopic treatment yet?

Kasi Lemmons: It definitely wasn't for lack of trying. It's hard to get any film made, and part of my career is that it's hard to get Black dramas made. Especially a Black period drama with a female protagonist. But that time has come. The powers that be are ready to see that there's an audience for Black female-driven movies. That should have been a no-brainer, but it's been a tricky contest.

We've been told over and over again that these things are very difficult to get an audience for. Part of what aligned the stars to get this one made is that we had a great actress attached, but I think its time has really come.

MM: Did you and cowriter Gregory Allen Howard work together, or did his script already exist and you rewrote it?

KL: Gregory was really ahead of his time. He first wrote the script twenty years ago. He tried to get the film made at Disney, and then about five years ago he approached (producer) Debra Martin Chase and said that he really wanted to get this film made. When they came to me two and a half years ago, it was with the understanding that I would rewrite the script, because it really hadn't been rewritten in twenty years. So I came to it with the mission of really trying to get to her womanhood.

MM: Did you have any conversations about whether it should be a movie, or if it should be a prestige TV miniseries?

KL: We didn't. We knew we wanted to do theatrical. That was the goal and the dream of the producers. And that was also something that Focus Features said to us: "Whatever you do, do it theatrical." That meant a lot to me, because we should be able to do this movie theatrical, and it should be able to get an audience. I wanted a movie that a sophisticated ten-year-old could see with his grandmother.

MM: Was the goal always to get it to two hours, or were there times where you imagined *Harriet* as a more expansive, *Malcolm X*-style epic?

KL: Well certainly I did once I started doing my research. My treatments were very long. So there was a process of honing it down to get it to a manageable length. And frankly, we shot a lot more. My first cut was much longer, as first cuts often are.

MM: Cynthia Erivo went from not having been in a film to suddenly being in several. When she became your target for *Harriet*, had she already been cast in *Widows* or *Bad Times at the El Royale*? Had she shot either of those films yet?

KL: I was introduced to Cynthia at my first meeting on *Harriet*. I knew (the producers) had been talking to somebody, and I don't know what I was expecting but I wasn't expecting to be impressed. But just looking at her told me they were serious. This was somebody who realistically could play Harriet Tubman. I knew of her even though I hadn't seen her on Broadway. But very quickly I could educate myself.

She was shooting *Widows* when I had my first meeting, and when I signed on she was shooting *El Royale*. So I didn't really start meeting Cynthia until I was diving into my research. That's when I started to have a really clear picture of who Harriet was, and who she was physically. And I could tell Cynthia had the fire in her to play the role.

MM: Cynthia had already won a Tony, and you knew she was a knockout of a singer. When did it first get broached for her to do a song for the film?
KL: She sings as Harriet in the movie, so we had already been listening to her and we had been talking about what purpose music had in the film, and in Harriet's life. It's not about prettiness, it's about communication. I was listening to a lot of demos from artists, and hearing some really great stuff but not quite hearing what connected to me, or to the old traditions I wanted to draw from. And then I heard a song written by Joshuah Campbell—the tribute he did to John Lewis—and I asked him for a demo and he did the first draft of the song. Then Cynthia came on and they wrote together.

MM: Your cinematographer, John Toll, is known for films like *Braveheart* and *The Last Samurai*—historical epics with a classical sense of heroism at the center. Is that deliberately what you were going for?
KL: Yes, it's certainly not a fluke that he came on *Harriet*. It's a small film by certain standards, but I wanted it to have a big movie feel. We were trying to make an audience-friendly film and I wanted it to have scope. I knew that was something he could deliver. Obviously John is a pro and a genius, and I was very lucky to get him.

MM: You've tended to work mostly with the same composer and editor (Terence Blanchard and Terilyn A. Shropshire, respectively), but often work with different cinematographers. Where do you find the balance between having continuity with your key collaborators or having new voices? And how do you decide which spots on the crew you want steadiness with and which spots are open to those new voices?
KL: I love working with people I've worked with before. I really adore it. But sometimes it's important to get out of that to see how everything holds up with different collaborators. I've worked with different cinematographers on most of my films, which is deliberate in some ways but in some ways is incidental. When I start to do a film I look at who's available and what kind of photography relates

to that specific film. I loved working with Stéphane (Fontaine) on *Talk To Me*—I think he's fantastic. And I love John Toll. But they're very different cinematographers and those two movies are very different in the types of camera movement that I wanted. It's a question of what the story really calls for, and of what I'm seeing when I'm imagining the movie.

MM: Your filmography perfectly switches back and forth between period pieces and contemporary-set films. Is that by design or something that you consciously think about?

KL: (Laughs) It's not something I consciously think about. I really do love period pieces, but I also really like contemporary pieces. It usually just starts with a character that I'm interested in or fall in love with. The period just becomes how the story tells itself to me. So it just depends.

MM: The one small complaint I had about *Harriet* was that I worried for a film about slavery, it didn't go far enough in showing the cruelty. Obviously that's a sensitive subject, and you also said you wanted to make a film that was more accessible to broad audiences than, say, *12 Years a Slave* or even *Django Unchained*. How did you find that balance without also shying away from the truth of the story you were telling?

KL: It's super important to talk about the violence of slavery, but there are different types of violence. I really wanted to talk about the violence of family separation and the choices that people had to make. I felt that a lot has been said, and very eloquently, in film language about the damage done to people's bodies. I really wanted to talk about family and the sacrifices that people made. It was very moving to me to find out about the stories just within her family—her sister not wanting to leave her children, her other sisters being sold away, and her brother leaving his wife in childbirth. Those stories were very important to me and it was a different kind of violence that I was interested in.

And even though I would never want to downplay cruelty in slavery, I was trying to talk about it in a different way. It wasn't about shying away from violence, even though at a certain point I realized I wanted kids to be able to see it. It seemed to me that it would be tragic to take the film away from young people. But it really wasn't shying away so much as I really did want to focus on the story of Harriet Tubman, her family, and the move toward freedom. That's what I think the Harriet Tubman story is—a freedom story.

Index

About the Editor

Christina N. Baker is associate professor of critical race studies at University of California, Merced. She is author of *Contemporary Black Women Filmmakers and the Art of Resistance*, the first book-length analysis of representations of Black femaleness in the feature films of Black women filmmakers. Her work has been published in such journals as *Sex Roles: A Journal of Research*; *Social Psychology of Education*; *Journal of College Student Development*; *The Urban Review: Issues and Ideas in Public Education*; and *Women, Gender, & Families of Color*.